THE EXTRAORDINARY JOURNEY

OF

MOSES

A Prophet tested by Pharaoh and later on by the Israelites

M. TARIQUL

First Edition: 2023

ISBN: 979-8-9894801-0-4

Cover photo credit: Munny Aktary

Moses, a prophet admired by the followers of three religions.

At his birth, he was destined to be killed by the soldiers of Pharaoh but eventually adopted by the family of Pharaoh.

Accidentally killed a man at a young age and went into exile for a number of years.

One night in the desert, climbed a mountain pursuing a light for guidance but ended up having a direct conversation with God.

Confronted the mighty Pharaoh as a messenger of God to rescue the Israelites from the horrific oppression.

But, after the exodus, life became more difficult due to the rebellious Israelites.

Died without realizing his dream of living in the promised land.

It's a book about the extraordinary life journey of Moses, where you also can know how the Children of Israel, who used to live in Canaan, ended up in Egypt in the first place.

CONTENTS

THE PHARAOH

In ancient Egypt, Pharaoh was the title for the ruler of their kingdom, and throughout much of ancient history, Egyptians followed polytheistic religions; they called the sun 'Ra' and worshipped it as their supreme deity. They believed that all Pharaohs were the descendants of the sun god, Ra.

Geographically, the Egyptian civilization developed along the Nile River mainly because the river's annual flooding ensured reliable, rich soil for growing crops.

During the birth and lifetime of Moses, there was a tyrant Pharaoh, who used to rule the kingdom by dividing the people into different classes in society. Among the population, ethnically there were two groups, Copts, the indigenous, and Israelites, who migrated from the Canaan region (present-day Palestine, Israel, Lebanon, Jordan, and Syria) around a century back.

Israelites were the descendants of the Prophet Israel (Jacob), the grandson of the Prophet Abraham. The religion of the Israelites was monotheistic; they believed in one God, as their forefather Prophet Abraham believed and preached.

Throughout history, Divide and rule has been an effective formula for any tyrant to cling to Power. A unified force is the biggest threat to their oppression and corruption. In a divided society, if one group can enjoy some undue benefit by oppressing the other group, they can never form a unified front that favors the tyrant ruler. Pharaoh used the same strategy during his reign.

Israelites were the people oppressed most by the Pharaoh; he enslaved and forced them to do all sorts of mean and hard work for the Coptic people and kingdom. Israelites did not have any human rights, let alone civil rights. They used to live in ghettos; their movements were restricted and monitored by the soldiers.

One day, Pharaoh had a dream in which he saw a fire emerge from the direction of present-day Jerusalem-Syria, which burnt all the Coptic people and their dwellings but did not harm the Israelites.

Pharaoh was deeply upset to have seen such a bizarre dream. He gathered all the priests, soothsayers, and sorcerers asked them to interpret the dream, to which they predicted,

"A boy will be born in the Israelites, who will cause the fall of your kingdom."

Upon listening to this, Pharaoh ordered to kill all the baby boys going to be born in the Israelites but spare the girls [1].

This utterly barbaric oppression continued for many years. Spies of Pharaoh used to monitor the pregnant women of the Israelites. When the babies were born, soldiers killed them immediately if it was a boy.

But killing all the newborn boy babies alarmed a new problem for the people and kingdom. They complained to the Pharaoh that there would be shortages of laborers in the future for the hard work, which the Coptic people did not or could not do. Hearing that complaint, the Pharaoh decided to kill the newborn boys every alternative year.

Killing thousands of newborn babies just for the fear of losing the kingship was the height of crossing any limit any tyrant could think of. Which just demonstrated what type of evil and oppressive mind the Pharaoh had.

The Coptic population of that time was equally guilty of that barbaric oppression. For their own livelihood and comfortable life, they not only agreed to enslave the Israelites but also supported the killing of the Israelites' babies by the Pharaoh.

And how helpless were the Israelites that they could not even protest against the killing of their newborn babies? Which continued for years.

BIRTH OF MOSES

The mother of Moses was pregnant, but she kept it hidden very carefully, and it was the year of killing. It may be easy to hide the pregnancy, but how can one conceal a newborn child?

So, when the baby Moses was born, God inspired in the mind of Moses's mother,

"Suckle him, but when you fear for him, cast him into the river, and do not fear or grieve. We will certainly return him to you" [2].

When a baby suckles and drinks his mother's milk for the first time, a connection and relation are established immediately between them. The Baby never forgets that taste of milk and the warm feeling of the mother's lap. Moreover, if the baby was hungry, naturally, it could cry, which might draw the attention of the Pharaoh's spies and soldiers. So, after suckling him, she did float baby Moses into the river.

A mother had to float her baby into a basket on a river like the Nile! What was her mental state at that time? She might have saved him from the soldiers of the Pharaoh, but his life was still in great danger. He might have drowned in the river or been attacked by crocodiles because, at that time, the Nile was the home of hippos and crocodiles.

With all those fears, she asked her daughter to follow the basket where it was going [3]. And she followed him very diligently, always keeping an eye on the floating basket but not as such that others' attention could be diverted to it, which might have endangered her brother's life. Quite an intelligent girl she was.

ADOPTED BY THE FAMILY OF PHARAOH

The basket carrying Moses floated all the way to the castle of Pharoh. Pharaoh's wife, Asiya, might be having leisure time near the blank of the river, noticed the basket and asked a slave to bring it to her. Pharaoh and Asiya did not have any babies. So, when she saw the cute baby Moses, she instinctively felt a sudden surge of love for him.

She knew very well what was supposed to happen with this baby, so she took baby Moses to the Pharaoh and said to him.

"This baby is a source of joy for me and you. Do not kill him; Perhaps he may be useful to us."

She tried to convince Pharaoh that when this cute baby grew up, he could help them as a slave. When she saw no rejection from her husband, she pushed for more by saying,

"We can adopt him as a son" [4]. Pharaoh agreed reluctantly.

As the Pharaoh agreed to adopt the baby, the infant Moses became the prince and he needed breastfeeding. Several wet nurses were engaged to breastfeed him, but he did not accept anyone's milk and kept crying. That caused them to look for new wet nurses.

Moses's sister was wandering outside the palace to know her brother's status. When some royal maids came out and were looking for wet nurses for a baby, she offered her help to them by suggesting,

"Shall I direct you to a family who will bring him up for you and take good care of him?" [5].

She directed them to her own house, but the maids did not know that. They took Moses's mother to the palace, and the baby happily suckled milk from her breast. This is how God fulfilled his promise made to Moses's mother by reuniting her with the baby [6].

The life of Moses was not only saved from Pharaoh's killing order but he was even adopted by the Pharaoh.

ACCIDENTALLY KILLED SOMEONE

Moses was a young and mature man then. God blessed him with intelligence and wisdom. He was growing up in the palace of the Pharoh, so naturally was aware of the affairs of the kingdom. As there were some noticeable differences in physical appearance and skin color between the Copts and the Israelites, Moses had the idea by that time to which racial group he belonged.

He used to visit the city and witnessed the cruelty with which the Israelites were treated. His praiseworthy qualities were doing good and helping others in need [7].

One day, he was walking around the city at a time when most of the people were taking a rest. Egypt was an extremely hot climate country, and generally, at noon, it was so hot that people could not stay outside that period of the day.

Around this time of the day, Moses saw two people fighting; one was a local Copts, and another one was an Israeli. He thought, like all the cases of the kingdom, here also a Coptic man oppressing an Israeli. So, he tried to help his own race man and, to save him, punched the Coptic guy. The locals could not tolerate the punch and died immediately.

When he saw the Egyptian fall down after receiving the blow and breathe his last,

Moses cried,

"This is from Satan's handiwork. He is certainly a sworn, misleading enemy." [8]

The state of utter remorse and confusion in which Moses uttered these words shows he had no intention to murder, nor was he expecting that the person would die on receiving a punch. He confessed to God that by following his rage, he actually followed the footsteps of the devil.

Moses realized he had committed a major sin by killing a human, so immediately prayed to God for forgiveness,

"My Master! I have definitely wronged my soul, so forgive me." [9].

The incident indicates Moses had a very kind heart, was ready to help someone he did not even know, and physically he was very strong. The Coptic man just died by one punch from him. But his physical strength did not make him arrogant; quite the opposite in fact. He was distressed that he had misused his strength, and with that guilty feeling, he was ready to ask for forgiveness from God immediately.

The following day, Moses was fearing whether anyone knew about his killing of the Coptic man. Like other days, when he entered the city, he saw the same Israeli man fighting with another Copts. Upon seeing Moses, the Israeli guy asked for help again. But this time, Moses realized this Israeli man was in fact a troublemaker.

Moses rebuked him,

"Indeed, you are clearly a troublemaker." [10].

But upon his continuous persuasion, when Moses finally moved forward to help, the Israeli guy thought this time Moses was coming to punish him, so to save himself,

He publicly shouted,

> "O Moses! Do you intend to kill me as you killed a man yesterday? You only want to be a tyrant in the land. You do not intend to make peace!" [11]

With that, everybody in the city got to know that Moses was the one who killed the Coptic person. It was a significant crime in their eyes because they knew that although Moses lived in the Pharaoh's Palace as a prince, he was actually an Israeli. So when they realized that Moses even dared to kill a Copts, they could not tolerate it.

The chiefs and ministers of the royal court conspired for Moses's death penalty. But there was a man who liked Moses and got to know about the ministers plotting. He rushed to Moses with that information and advised him to leave the country immediately,

He said to him,

> "O Moses! The chiefs are actually conspiring against you to put you to death, so leave the city." [12].

EXILE TO THE MIDIAN REGION

Moses left the country to the unknown with great fear and asked for help from God by praying,

"My Master, deliver me from these unjust people." [13],

And when reached a region named Midian, he said to himself,

"I trust my Master will guide me to the right way." [14].

There, he went to a well for water and saw people watering their herds, but two women were holding their herds with some difficulty. When Moses asked them about their problem, they replied

"We cannot water our herds until the other shepherds are done, for our father is a very old man." [15].

So, he watered their herd for them, withdrew to the shade, and prayed to God,

"My Master! I am truly in desperate need of whatever provision You may have in store for me" [16].

After that long journey, which must have caused Moses much mental and physical fatigue, he still did not hesitate to help someone in need. And his prayer to God was so genuine; he was in complete submission to God's mercy and would be happy for any provision.

The girls went home and told everything to their father, who might realize that this unknown person (Moses) had a good character and kind heart. He sent one of his daughters to Moses.

She told him,

"My father is inviting you so he may reward you for watering our animals for us."

When Moses came to the old man and told him his whole story,

The old man said,

"Have no fear! You are now safe from the wrongdoing, people." [17]

He assured Moses that the Midian region was not under the kingdom ruled by Pharaoh. His daughters were listening to the conversion and might be impressed by the Moses character and his stories.

One of the two daughters suggested,

"O my dear father! Hire him. A strong, trustworthy person is definitely the best to hire." [18]

Her father had a better idea; he offered a marriage proposal for one of his daughters to Moses,

"I wish to marry one of these two daughters of mine to you, provided that you stay in my service for eight years. If you complete ten, it will be a favor from you, but I do not wish to make it difficult for you. God willing, you will find me an agreeable man." [19]

Moses responded,

"Then it is settled between you and I. Whichever term I fulfill, there will be no further obligation on me. And God is a Witness to what we say." [20]

Moses got a place to live, a job to survive, and a family with an identity. What a turn in life! A few moments back, he was a fugitive and homeless person, but the next moment, he got everything he needed. What a huge change a simple good act can make in life!

DIRECT CONVERSATION WITH GOD

When Moses completed the term and was traveling with his family, he spotted a flicker of light on the side of Mount Sinai. So he said to his family,

"Stay here, for I have spotted a fire. Perhaps from there, I can bring you some directions or a torch from the fire so you may warm yourselves." [21] [22]

In the middle of a journey and at night time, they might feel some vulnerability. They might feel lost in the desert, the coldness of the weather, and fear of attack from night animals.

So, when Moses spotted a flicker of light on a mountain, he wanted to pursue that, hoping to get some directions about the path from the people around there or at least get a torch of fire that could give his family some warmth and safety from the attack of night animals.

Eventually, when he came to it, he was called from the bush to the right side of the valley,

"O Moses! It is truly I. I am God - the Master of all dominion." [23]

"So, take off your sandals, for you are in the sacred valley of Tuwa." [24]

In the middle of the night, on top of a mountain valley, a light source called him by his name! It must have baffled Moses.

So, God was assuring him,

"I have chosen you, so listen to what is revealed" [25]

God assured him not to be worried; he was chosen for a purpose, and he better listen carefully to what was going to be revealed.

God reaffirmed his authority and right to be worshiped alone only, by saying,

"It is truly I. I am God! There is no god worthy of worship except Me. So, worship Me alone, and establish prayer for My remembrance." [26]

Israelites were the descendants of Prophet Israel, the grandson of Prophet Abraham, who believed and preached the religion of One God. So, being an Israeli, Moses had that belief.

He also witnessed injustice and oppression by the people, especially by the Pharaoh in Egypt. So, he might have thought that when the accountability and justice would occur for these oppressions?

God answered that thought by saying to Moses,

"The Hour is sure to come. My will is to keep it hidden so that every soul may be rewarded according to their efforts." [27]

Judgment day will surely occur; it is inevitable, but God has kept the date hidden from the people. So, some may restrain themselves from doing anything wrong for the fear of being judged one day, and some may not believe in it and do whatever they desire. But eventually, everyone will be rewarded or punished for their efforts.

God continued,

> "So do not let those who disbelieve in it and follow their desires distract you from it, or you will be doomed." [28]

God was advising Moses that he should not be distracted by the carefree lifestyle of the wrongdoers. They might have had an easy and lavish life then, but eventually, they were destined to be doomed, especially on the Judgment Day. After all those heavy talks, God wanted to ease Moses,

So he asked,

> "And what is that in your right hand, O Moses?" [29]

Moses replied,

> "It is my staff! I lean on it, and with it, I beat down branches for my sheep and have other uses for it." [30]

God asked him,

> "Throw it down, O Moses!" [31]

So, he did; it became a serpent, slithering [32]. When he saw it slithering like a snake, he ran away without looking back.

God assured him,

> "O Moses! Draw near, and have no fear. You are perfectly secure." [33]".

> "We will return it to its former state [34]."

When Moses held the snake, it became his usual stick again.

God then asked Moses,

> "And put your hand under your armpit; it will come out shining white, unblemished, as another sign." [35]

> "So that We may show you some of Our greatest signs." [36]

A stick that could change into a giant snake, and a hand that could come out in shining white color, were not normal things people had ever heard of. Those are only possible for God, and Moses might have wondered why God was showing those divine signs to him.

God explained,

> "These are two proofs from your Master to Pharaoh and his chiefs. They have truly been a rebellious people." [37]

God commanded Moses to go to the Pharaoh and his people with these signs; so that they could understand that the message Moses was conveying to them was indeed from God. From that point in time, Moses (peace be upon him) became the Messenger of God.

Moses understood his responsibility and also the challenges he could face in this mission.

So he said,

> "My Master! I fear that they will reject me." [38]

and added,

> "My Master! I have indeed killed a man from them, so I fear they may kill me." [39]

He continued,

> "And my brother Aaron is more eloquent than I, so send him with me as a helper to support what I say, for I truly fear they may reject me." [40]

God responded,

> "We will assist you with your brother and grant you both authority so they cannot harm you. With Our signs, you and those who follow you will certainly prevail." [41]

Moses then prayed,

> "My Master! Uplift my heart for me, [42]
> and make my task easy, [43]
> and remove the impediment from my tongue, [44]
> so people may understand my speech, [45]

In an argument, an authoritative person can impose a psychological effect on his counterpart. Tightness in the chest and loss of words are the mental challenges one typically faces in that situation. So, an intelligent man like Moses correctly understood what sort of psychological challenges he had to overcome to deliver a clear message, that people could understand. And who else can remove those challenges for him other than God!

God responded,

"All that you requested has been granted, O Moses! [46]

God then reminded Moses that this was not the first time he did favor on him.

God said to Moses,

"And surely We had shown you favor before" [47]

"When We inspired your mother with this: [48]

"Put him into a chest, then put it into the river. The river will wash it ashore, and he will be taken by Pharaoh, an enemy of Mine and his. And I endeared you with love from Me, O Moses so that you would be brought up under My watchful Eye." [49]

"Remember,

when your sister came along and proposed, 'Shall I direct you to someone who will nurse him?' So, We reunited you with your mother so that her heart would be put at ease and she would not grieve. Later, you killed a man by mistake, but We saved you from sorrow, as well as other tests We put you through. Then you stayed for a number of years among the people of Midian. Then you came here as pre-destined, O Moses!" [50]

God had been preparing Moses [51] to be a Messenger with a mission where confronting the Pharaoh was the first task, but guiding the

Israelites was the primary job he was about to conduct in the following days. And by reminding him of all those favors, God assured Moses that he was with him all along his life and was in complete control of everything, so he should not fear any harm from anyone as long as he followed the commands of God.

God commanded Moses, which implied to his brother, Prophet Aaron also,

> "So go to Pharaoh and say,
>
> 'Indeed, we are both messengers from your Master, so let the children of Israel go with us, and do not oppress them. We have come to you with a sign from your Master. And salvation will be for whoever follows the right guidance.' [52]
>
> "It has indeed been revealed to us that the punishment will be upon whoever denies the truth and turns away." [53]

God also commanded them not to be harsh on Pharaoh at first,

> "Speak to him gently, so perhaps he may be mindful of Me or fearful of My punishment." [54]

There is a way to convey the message of God, even to a person who was an oppressor like the Pharaoh. So the oppressor or wrongdoer could understand the consequences of the actions he was involved in and had the opportunity to amend himself. That command was a pure mercy from God.

CONFRONTATION WITH PHARAOH

Moses and his brother prophet Aaron went to the royal court and conveyed the message of God to the Pharaoh and his ministers. Moses advised the Pharaoh to submit himself to the will of One God and let the Israelites free and go with him. But Pharaoh was an evil genius and skilled politician; he ignored the message Moses conveyed and tried to demean him from an emotional perspective.

He said to Moses,

> "Did we not raise you among us as a child, and you stayed several years of your life in our care?" [55]

Pharaoh wanted to frame Moses as ungrateful by saying he adopted and raised him, but in return, Moses was challenging his authority. When someone doesn't have the answer to a legitimate demand, then they try to play an emotional or psychological game to win the argument. Pharaoh had the same policy.

Moses replied to Pharaoh,

> "How can that be a favor, of which you remind me, when it was only because you have enslaved the Israelites?" [56]

Moses' argument to the Pharaoh's emotional play was, how can he justify the killings of thousands of newborn babies of the Israelites by adopting one child of them?

Pharaoh had no logical reply to that argument, so he tried to demean Moses by imposing a guilty consciousness on him.

He said to Moses,

"Then you did what you did." [57]

Pharaoh indirectly reminded Moses that he killed a Coptic man and then ran away.

Moses replied,

"I did it then, lacking guidance." [58]

"So, I fled from you when I feared you. Then my Master granted me wisdom and made me one of the messengers." [59]

Pharaoh thought Moses would be afraid to talk about that issue, but by acknowledging the killing, Moses directly addressed that. He argued that he did not know how to deal with the matter then, so he fled to save his life. But he had no fear of Pharaoh and his army anymore; he only had the fear of God. So, to obey the command of God, he was ready to face his past and rescue the Israelites from the oppression of Pharaoh.

Pharaoh understood that his initial tactics to divert the argument to a different direction had failed, so he reluctantly decided to address the message of Moses.

Pharaoh asked,

"Who then is the Master of you two, O Moses?" [60]

"And what is the Master of all dominions?" [61]

Moses answered,

"Our Master is the One Who has given everything its distinctive form, then guided it." [62]

"He is the Master of the heavens and the earth and everything in between, if only you had sure faith." [63]

Copts used to worship the Sun as the ruler of the sky/haven, and believed Pharaoh had the right to rule the earth as the descendant of the sun. By one statement, Moses clarified that there is only one God, who is the true Master of the sky and earth: the total dominion. He also reminded them that God is the one who created them and gave them their physical shapes. Likewise, the sky, earth, and everything in between are the creations of God; he is the only Master of all of these.

Pharaoh said to those around him,

"Did you hear what he said?" [64]

He tried to provoke the Ministers and other people of the royal court by saying Moses was humiliating their sun god.

Moses ignored and continued by saying,

"He is your Master and the Master of your forefathers." [65]

Moses double-downed his message by saying that God is not only their Master but also the Master of their ancestors.

In reply, Pharaoh said mockingly,

"Indeed, your messenger, who has been sent to you, is insane." [66]

Pharaoh tried to humiliate Moses by mocking his claim to be a messenger of God. But Moses did not pay any attention to that and continued his message by saying,

"He is the Master of the east and west, and everything in between, if only you had any sense." [67]

Moses shifted his attention from the Pharaoh to the people of the royal court and explained to them that if they used their senses, they could clearly understand that the sun is controlled by someone else. It always rises from the east and sets in the west; if the sun was the god, it could have risen from any side and set on any side of the sky it wished.

Moses continued,

"He is the One Who has laid out the earth for all of you, and set in its pathways for you, and sends down rain from the sky, causing various types of plants to grow" [68]

Every year, the Nile River flooded the land and brought black soil with it, which made the land of Egypt very fertile. When rain dropped from the sky and moistened the fertile land, various crops used to grow there. Moses explained to them that all these provisions were from God. Those who have sound judgment could see these signs.

Pharaoh realized that Moses ignored and overcame his tactics of personal humiliation and got the people's attention with his compelling message, so he tried to mock Moses' claim of having a conversation with God on a mountain.

Pharaoh declared,

> "O chiefs! I know of no other god for you but myself. So, bake bricks out of clay for me, O Haman, and build a high tower so I may look at the God of Moses, although I am sure he is a liar." [69]

He tried to reimpose his divine status to the people around him because if they started to believe Moses' message of one God, then he would be doomed. By the way, Haman was the minister in charge of the construction works of the kingdom.

Pharaoh then threatened Moses,

> "If you take any other god besides me, I will certainly have you imprisoned." [70]

He indirectly threatened the people of the court that if they desired to follow Moses, prison would be their destination.

Moses responded,

> "Even if I bring you a clear proof?" [71]

Pharaoh demanded,

> "Bring it then, if what you say is true." [72]

In reply, Moses threw his stick, and it became a giant snake [73]. And then he drew his hand out, and it was shining white [74].

So far, everyone in the royal court was listening to the undeniable arguments of Moses, but when they witnessed the unimaginable signs, God granted for Moses, they got rattled at their core.

A giant snake slithering in the ground of the royal court! Quite a horrible experience for the people present there. And when they saw Moses's shining white hand, they were just speechless.

Pharaoh realized his kingship and his false divine status were under serious threat. At that time, if he had decided to kill or imprison Moses, people might have considered him a hero and might have even started to follow him as a messenger of God.

So, he tried to discredit the signs Moses was showing in the royal court. He said to the chiefs around him,

"He is indeed a skilled magician" [75]

"Who seeks to drive you from your land by his magic. So, what do you propose?" [76]

Patriotism card is a very effective tactic for a ruler. Pharaoh played it with his ministers. He wanted to tell them that if they started to believe Moses as a messenger, then the enslaved Israelites had to be free, who would then overcome them in their own kingdom; the tactic worked.

The ministers replied,

"Let him and his brother wait and dispatch mobilizers to all cities." [77]

"To bring you every skilled magician." [78]

Pharaoh liked the idea and said to Moses,

> "We can surely meet you with similar magic. So set for us an appointment that neither of us will fail to keep, in a central place." [79]

Moses said,

> "Your appointment is on the Day of the Festival, and let the people be gathered mid-morning." [80]

Ministers' advice to Pharaoh was to gather all the top-rated magicians of the kingdom and have a competition with Moses. They did not consider the signs Moses showed as divine; they thought it was just like other magics they used to know. So, they were confident that their top magicians could defeat Moses and restore the Coptic people's superiority in the religion and kingdom. Pharaoh liked the advice and invited Moses for a showdown with his selected magicians.

Moses agreed and suggested the competition should be arranged in the open, in a festival gathering where general citizens of the kingdom could witness it. He wanted to use that opportunity to reach more people with the message of One God.

.

SHOWDOWN WITH THE MAGICIANS

From all over the kingdom, Pharaoh gathered a number of top-rated magicians and trained them for a period. In the meantime, news about what happened in the royal court spread everywhere in the kingdom. The credibility of the Pharaoh, who had a divine status to the citizens, was under serious threat.

The kingship of Pharaoh was based on the belief that he was the descendant of sun god. In the showdown between Moses and the gathered magicians, if it had been proved that the message of Moses was real, which was "there is only One God who creates and controls everything," then Pharoh would lose not only his status of divinity but also his kingship.

This made the magicians the most influential men in the kingdom then; everyone's attention was on them. So much so that people even started to talk that they would follow the magicians instead of the Pharoh if they could win against Moses.

The people were asked,

"Will you join the gathering?" [81]

"So that we may follow the magicians if they prevail" [82]

Magicians understood their newfound influential status, so they tried to get some benefit from it.

They asked Pharaoh,

"Shall we have a suitable reward if we prevail?" [83]

Pharaoh replied,

"Yes, and you will then certainly be among those closest to me." [84]

From the reply of the Pharaoh, the magicians thought they would get some ministerial post in the royal court and with it, all the access to power and wealth.

In any society, people closest to the ruler have the most influence in terms of power, authority, and wealth. When the ruler was like Pharaoh, one of the most powerful in the world at that time, then this access and position became more lucrative.

On the scheduled date, people from all over the country gathered in the place where Moses and the magicians were about to face off. Moses and his brother Aaron were on one side and the magicians were on the other.

Moses warned the magicians,

"Do not fabricate a lie against God, or He will wipe you out with a torment." [85]

Moses warned the magicians that by participating in the competition they were trying to deny God's divine sign, for which God's punishment would be severe.

But after some discussion among themselves, the magicians replied, [86]

"These two are only magicians who want to drive you out of your land with their magic, and do away with your most cherished traditions." [87]

Magicians were in the dream of getting ministerial posts from the Pharaoh; They could not think of anything that might blow that chance. So, they told the people what Pharaoh wanted them to say.

The competition started; the magicians said,

"O Moses! Either you throw, or let us be the first to throw." [88]

Moses responded,

"No, you go first."

The magicians threw their staffs, and suddenly their ropes and staffs seemed to move like snakes [89]. It was so overwhelming that even Moses had fear in his mind [90].

But God assured him,

"Do not fear! It is certainly you who will prevail." [91]

"Throw what is in your right hand, and it will swallow up what they have made, for what they have made is no more than a magic trick. And magicians can never succeed wherever they go." [92]

Magic does not matter how overwhelming it seems; in the end it is just magic, made of illusion by man-made tricks. It can never compete with divine signs. The same thing happened there also.

When Moses threw down his staff, it became the giant snake that immediately swallowed all the objects of their illusion! [93].

The whole crowd witnessed that the competition had just ended before it began; they were just stunned.

By witnessing that, the magicians fell down in prostration and declared, [94]

"We now believe in the Master of all dominion" [95]

"The Master of Moses and Aaron." [96]

The magicians clearly understood what they had just witnessed was not magic. If nobody else, they surely knew what was magic and what was not. Their whole life spent practicing magic and reaching such a position that even Pharaoh called them for a competition of that magnitude.

So, when the truth became clear to them, they could not hold themselves but prostrate to the One God and declare their belief.

Pharaoh gathered these top-rated magicians and arranged a festival event so people could come out to witness the competition, where he thought Moses would be defeated and humiliated in front of everyone. But things just went in the opposite direction.

He became furious with the magicians; first of all, they lost; then they even prostrated and declared their belief in front of the crowd.

Pharaoh threatened them,

"How dare you believe in him before I give you permission?"

"He must be your master who taught you magic."

Pharaoh was an evil genius; to save his face in front of the crowd, he invented a lie and accused the magicians of having a pre-pact plan with Moses.

He even tried to turn them around from their just declared belief by threatening,

"Soon you will see. I will certainly cut off your hands and feet on opposite sides, then crucify you all." [97]

If a person's one hand and one foot is cut off, then he neither can hold anything nor will be able to stand; what an evil torture it was by the Pharaoh!

The magicians responded to the threat of Pharaoh,

"By the One Who created us! We will never prefer you over the clear proofs that have come to us. So do whatever you want! Your authority only covers this worldly life." [98]

Few moments back, for their greed of power and wealth, the magicians were ready to do anything to please the Pharaoh. But in the next moment when the truth became clear to them, they were ready to tolerate the horrible torture the Pharaoh had threatened them. They were even ready to accept death by crucifixion but not ready to leave the truth. The power of truth is just unimaginable; when people hold to the truth, nothing can fear them.

The last word of the magician was,

> "Indeed, we have believed in our Master so He may forgive our sins and that magic you have forced us to practice. And God is far superior in reward and more lasting in punishment." [99]

END OF PHARAOH AND HIS KINGDOM

After that humiliating defeat in front of the citizens, the ministers asked Pharaoh if he was considering freeing the Israelites.

"Are you going to leave Moses and his people free to spread corruption in the land and abandon you and your gods?" [100]

The fate of the ministers was also connected to the future of the Pharaoh. If the people started to believe the message of Moses and leave the false god like Pharaoh, ministers would also lose their power and influence in the society. Moreover, they feared that if the Israelites got freedom, they might avenge them.

Pharaoh understood their point and responded,

"Kill the sons of those who believe with him and keep their women." [101]

Previously, the state policy was to kill newborn boys every other year, but from then, a new verdict was given to kill the sons of the Israelites who would believe the message of Moses.

And Pharaoh added,

> "Let me kill Moses, and let him call upon his Master! I truly fear that he may change your traditions or cause mischief in the land." [102]

Pharaoh was pursuing his ministers not to think about the message of Moses otherwise they would lose their traditions and superiority in the land. He also understood that Moses might have some effect on his ministers, which became true in the next moment.

One of his ministers argued,

> "Will you kill a man only for saying: 'My Master is one' while he has in fact come to you with clear proofs from your Master?
>
> If he is a liar, it will be to his own loss. But if he is truthful, then you will be afflicted with some of what he is threatening you with." [103]

He turned his attention to other ministers and said,

> "O my people! Authority belongs to you today, reigning supreme in the land. But who would help us against the torment of God, if it were to befall us?" [104]

Hearing the speech, Pharaoh understood his own cabinet might get against him. And after that humiliation by the magicians in front of the people, the ministers might not fear him that much also.

So, he tried to assure them,

"I am telling you only what I believe, and I am leading you only to the way of guidance." [104]

But the believing man did not stop to convince the other members and reminded them of the history of past generations and their fates,

"O my people! I truly fear for you the doom of earlier enemy forces" [105]

"Like the fate of the people of Noah, Aad, Thamud, and those after them." [106]

He also warned them about the judgment day,

"O my people! I truly fear for you the Day all will be crying out to each other" [107]

"The Day you will try in vain to turn your backs and run away, with no one to protect you from God." [108]

He even reminded them about the Prophet Joseph, who lived among them around a century back and preached the same message Moses was preaching.

"Joseph already came to you earlier with clear proofs, yet you never ceased to doubt what he came to you with. When he died, you said, 'God will never send a messenger after him." [109]

He urged,

"O my people! Follow me, and I will lead you to the Way of Guidance." [110]

He tried to convince his fellow ministers that if they were not comfortable to follow Moses, an Israeli, then they could trust him as he belonged to their own race.

He kept pursuing them by saying,

"O my people! This worldly life is only a fleeting enjoyment, whereas the Hereafter is truly the home of settlement." [111]

"O my people! How is it that I invite you to salvation, while you invite me to the Fire!" [112]

"You invite me to disbelieve in God and associate with Him what I have no knowledge of, while I invite you to the Almighty, Most Forgiving." [113]

"There is no doubt that whatever idols you invite me to worship are not worthy to be invoked either in this world or the Hereafter. Undoubtedly, our return is to God, and the transgressors will be the inmates of the Fire." [114]

After all those arguments, when he saw no change of position from the opposite side, the person understood his fate and said,

"You will remember what I say to you, and I entrust my affairs to God. Surely God is All-Seeing of all His servants." [115]

There, the Israelites got the news that the Pharaoh had ordered to kill the sons of those who would believe and follow Moses. By hearing the news, the Israelites understood they were in greater danger than the past times.

But Moses reassured his people,

"Seek God's help and be patient. Indeed, the earth belongs to him alone. He grants it to whoever He chooses of His servants. The ultimate outcome belongs only to the righteous." [116]

But they complained,

"We have always been oppressed, before and after you came to us with the message." [117]

Moses replied,

"Perhaps your Master will destroy your enemy and make you successors in the land to see what you will do." [117]

God answered Moses's prayer. For ten years Pharaoh tried to kill Moses but could not. God afflicted Pharaoh's people with famine and shortage of crops so they might come back to their senses. [118]

God plagued them with floods, locusts, lice, frogs, and blood as clear signs, but they persisted in arrogance and were wicked. [119]

These punishments came in the form of floods that demolished their dwellings, swarms of locusts that destroyed the crops, pestilence of lice that made their life miserable, frogs that croaked and sprang everywhere, and the turning of all drinking water into blood. In times of prosperity, they said,

"This is what we deserve," but in adversity, they blamed it on Moses and those with him. [120]

They blamed Moses was doing magic spells on them and said to him,

> "No matter what sign you may bring to deceive us, we will never believe in you." [121]

When tormented, they pleaded,

> "O Moses! Pray to your Master on our behalf, by virtue of the covenant He made with you." [122]

> "If you help remove this torment from us, we will certainly believe in you and let the Children of Israel go with you." [122]

But as soon as God removed the torment from them, they broke their promise [123]. They thought they could keep doing this deception forever. Pharaoh and his people got so drowned in their arrogance that did not realize, their end had arrived.

God inspired Moses, saying,

> "Leave with My servants at night, for you will surely be pursued." [124]

Hearing the news, Pharaoh sent mobilizers to all cities [125] and said,

> "These outcasts are just a handful of people, [126]"
> "Who have really enraged us" [127]
> "But we are all on the alert." [128]

They pursued them at sunrise. [129] When the two groups came face to face, the companions of Moses cried out,

> "We are overtaken for sure." [130]

When Moses and the Israelites reached the shore of the sea, Pharaoh and his army were behind them. Israelites feared there was no way to escape the Pharaoh's army, but Moses was a firm believer in God.

Moses reassured them,

> "Absolutely not! My Master is certainly with me, He will guide me." [131]

God inspired Moses,

> "Strike the sea with your staff,"
> and the sea was split; each part was like a huge mountain. [132]

By the command of God, when Moses struck the sea with his stick, the sea became divided, water was separated and the sea bed was surfaced to be used as a path.

Moses, along with the Israelites, went to the path, Pharaoh and his army followed them there [133].

Moses and the children of Israel reached the other side of the sea to the land [134]. But the Pharaoh and all his army drowned in the sea [135].

It was one of the greatest signs from God for mankind. A sea that was divided to make a path for the believers; the same sea caused the destruction of the mightiest king and his army of that era.

ISRAELITES GOT THE FREEDOM

After so many years of that terrible oppression by the Pharaoh in Egypt, the Children of Israel were finally free. They were no longer enslaved and forced to live in ghettos; no threats of killing their newborn sons anymore. That was how God fulfilled his promise, which Moses conveyed to the Israelites [117] [136].

But that freedom and blessings did not make the Children of Israel grateful to God; instead, they walked in the opposite direction. When the Israelites came to the land on the other side of the sea, the present-day Sinai Peninsula, they came upon a people devoted to idols. And Israelites, being enslaved by the Copts for such a long time and thus considerably influenced by their culture, felt the desire to indulge in idol worship.

They demanded,

"O Moses! Make for us a god like their gods."

Moses replied,

"Indeed, you are a people acting ignorantly! [137]

Moses was shocked that after seeing all those signs from God, who just saved them by parting the sea and drowning the mighty Pharaoh along with his army, the Israelites could be that ignorant, who demanded idol worshipping!

He continued,

"What they follow is certainly doomed to destruction and their deeds are in vain." [138]

Moses warned them that whoever would follow the path of idol worship would have the same fate as the Pharaoh.

He added,

"Shall I seek for you a God other than the One, while He has honored you above the others?" [139]

He reminded all of them that God had honored them by granting freedom from the Pharaoh, which their earlier generations did not get.

BLESSED FOOD AND WATER FOR THE ISRAELITES

After crossing the sea, the children of Israel reached the Sinai Peninsula, which was a desert; there were no trees for shade and no vegetation as food. Moreover, the scorching heat of the desert was threatening to their survival. But God blessed the Children of Israel with ever-present clouds above them in the sky, which shaded and protected them in that desert from the heat of the sun. [140]

God also sent down to them a unique meal, Manna and Quails. [140]

Manna was a grain food. At night, dew used to fall from the clouds and the divine food, Manna also used to fall with it. It was like coriander seed, white in color and the taste was like wafers made with honey.

And Quails was a kind of bird. There were plenty of Quails available for the Israelites, so much so that the entire nation was able to live on them.

The human body needs carbohydrates and protein as two primary food content to survive. How merciful was God to the Israelites that he blessed them both, Manna as carbohydrates and Quails as protein in that desert.

And when the Israelites asked for water, God commanded Moses,

"Strike the rock with your staff." [140]

As another miraculous sign from God, twelve springs gushed out from the rock for twelve tribes. Each tribe chose a spring as their drinking place.

Had these divine provisions not been blessed by God for the thousands of Israelites, they would have certainly perished in that scorching desert.

REVELATION OF THE TORAH

Israelites were beginning their life as an independent nation and needed law to govern themselves. So, Moses was summoned by God to Mount Sinai so that he might receive the law for the children of Israel.

Initially, the appointment was for thirty nights; he had to devote himself to the worship of God by praying and fasting in sacculation so that he could develop the ability to receive the revelation which might put a heavy burden upon him.

Before leaving, Moses asked his brother Aaron,

> "Take my place among my people, do what is right, and do not follow the way of the corruptors." [141]

This indicates he already had the idea that there were some among the children of Israel who were troublemakers and may spread corruption or disturbance in the nation.

Moses might have felt some urgency and wanted to receive the law from God sooner so that he could guide his nation. He reached Mount Sinai ten days earlier than his appointed date. When he reached there,

God asked him,

> "O Moses, what has made you come in haste from your people?" [142]

He replied,

> "They are close on my tracks. And I have hastened to You, my Master, so You will be pleased." [143]

Moses was surprised to hear the question; he thought God would be happy that he showed up earlier. He also tried to explain to God that the Israelites were not that far from Mount Sinai.

But God said to him,

> "We have indeed tested your people in your absence, and the Samiri has led them astray." [144]

God was implying to Moses that, as a leader of a nation, he had a responsibility to the citizens, which should not be compromised. The most destructive thing that can happen to a nation is misguidance in the absence of a leader.

[More details about the matter of Samiri are discussed in the next chapter.]

Initially, God appointed Moses thirty nights for the worship but as he showed up ten days early, God made it forty nights. [141]

Direct conversation with God must be one of the greatest honor a human can ask for and Moses was having that honor for the second time. But he wished for more; he wanted to see God.

He asked,

> "My Master! Reveal Yourself to me so I may see You."

God answered,

> "You cannot see Me! But look at the mountain. If it remains firm in its place, only then will you see Me."

When his Master appeared to the mountain, it leveled to dust and Moses collapsed unconscious.

When he recovered, he cried,

> "Glory be to You! I turn to You in repentance and I am the first of the believers." [145]

Moses was already a believer in One God, but after that incident, he understood and believed that it is not possible for a human to see God in this world, so he immediately repented for crossing his limit by asking that.

God said to Moses,

> "O Moses! I have already elevated you above all others by My messages and speech. So hold firmly to what I have given you and be grateful." [146]

God explained to Moses that he should not feel sad as he already had an honor that others had not, to have direct conversation with God. And by receiving the holy tablet, the Torah from God, his rank had been elevated more.

Torah was revealed to Moses in written form, where the fundamentals of all the commandments were mentioned and explained for the children of Israel.

God commanded Moses,

> "Hold to this firmly and ask your people to take the best of it. I will soon show all of you the home of the rebellious. [147]

God commanded the Israelites to firmly believe the commandments revealed in the Torah and tried to follow those laws to the best of their abilities.

"Home of rebellious", by that phrase, the Israelites were told that on their way, they would come across the ruins of earlier nations who had refused to turn to God and who had persisted in their evil ways by denying the law or misinterpreting the law.

After the revelation of the Torah, that was a clear warning from God to the Children of Israel on how to follow the law of the Torah.

ISRAELITES WORSHIPED A GOLDEN CALF

While crossing the sea from Egypt to the Sinai Peninsula Israelites brought some of the jewelry of Copts with them. Those jewelry was made of gold. In the absence of Moses, they molded the jewelry and made an idol of a golden calf. When air passed between the opening of the mouth and tail of that calf, a lowing sound was heard and people around tried to claim that it was alive.

How absurd was that claim! Did they not see that it could neither speak to them nor guide them to the right Path? Still, they took it as a god! [148]

Aaron had warned them,

"O my people! You are only being tested by this, for indeed your one true Master is the Most Compassionate. So follow me and obey my orders." [149]

But they replied,

"We will not cease to worship it until Moses returns to us." [150]

As Moses was in sacculation for forty days on Mount Sinai, and was preparing to receive the Torah from God, Aaron was in charge of the Israelites and he warned them not to be misguided by worshiping the idol of golden calf. But they ignored his words and indirectly implied that he was not their leader; they would only listen to Moses.

When Moses returned and saw that idol worshiping, he was furious and at the same time, extremely sad. The grievous sin committed by the Israelites made him furious and their heedlessness made him very sad. As a messenger of God to the Israelites, he also might have felt leadership failure from his side.

He said,

"O my people! Had your Master not made you a good promise?"

"Has my absence been too long for you?"

"Or have you wished for wrath from your Master to befall you, so you broke your promise to me?" [151]

Moses reminded them that God fulfilled his promise by granting them freedom from the Pharaoh, which they thought would never occur.

He was surprised that how in just forty days of his absence they forgot the blessings God granted by rescuing them from the decades of slavery and torture.

Moses was even shocked to think how dare the Israelites were to break the promise with him after had witnessed the consequences of the same action by the Pharaoh and his people.

They argued,

> "We did not break our promise to you of our own free will, but we were made to carry the burden of the people's golden jewelry, then we threw it into the fire, and so did the Samiri." [152]

Then he molded for them an idol of a calf that made a lowing sound. They said,

> "This is your god and the god of Moses, but Moses forgot where it was!" [153]

Israelite leaders told Moses that Samiri was the master planner of the worshiping of the golden calf. He was the one who took all their gold pieces of jewelry, molded them, and shaped that as a calf.

Some people among the Israelites might have raised objections against the act in the name of Moses, but Samiri and his followers tried to convince them by saying that the idol of the golden calf was the forgotten god of Moses.

Moses commented to them,

> "What an evil thing you committed in my absence!" [154]

He threw down the Tablets and grabbed his brother by the hair, dragging him closer. [154]

Aaron pleaded,

> "O son of my mother! The people overpowered me and were about to kill me. So do not humiliate me and make my enemies rejoice, nor count me among the wrongdoing people." [154]

Aaron explained to Moses that he tried to prevent them from the idol worshiping but those Israelites were not in his control; things were so out of control that they even threatened to kill him.

Moses scolded his brother,

"O Aaron! What prevented you, when you saw them going astray," [155]

"From following after me? How could you disobey my orders?" [156]

Aaron pleaded,

"I really feared that you would say, 'You have caused division among the Children of Israel, and did not observe my word." [157]

Aaron wanted to say that, in that situation, people were divided into two camps; if he had been killed by the Idol worshiper's camp then civil war might have broken out among the Israelites for that crime, which might be more disappointing for Moses.

After hearing everything from the people and from his brother Aaron, Moses then turned his attention to the main culprit, Saimiri.

Moses asked,

"What did you think you were doing, O Samiri?" [158]

He said,

"I saw what they did not see, so I took a handful of dust from the hoof-prints of the horse of the messenger-angel Gabriel and then cast it on the molded calf". This is what my lower self tempted me into." [159]

Moses said,

"Go away then! And for the rest of your life, you will surely be crying, 'Do not touch me!'"

"Then you will certainly have a fate that you cannot escape."

"Now look at your god to which you have been devoted: we will burn it up, then scatter it in the sea completely." [160]

Moses understood that Samiri had just fabricated a story and said baseless words to justify his actions; any logical or intellectual argument with him would be in vain. So he just left him alone and cursed him for his grievous sin.

Moses then addressed his people,

"Your only god is One God, there is no god worthy of worship except Him. He encompasses everything in His knowledge." [161]

Moses prayed to God

"My Master! Forgive me and my brother! And admit us into Your mercy. You are the Most Merciful of the merciful." [162]

When Moses' anger subsided, he took up the Tablets. [163]

PUNISHMENT FOR THE IDOL WORSHIPING

Later, when the Israelites were filled with remorse and realized they had gone astray, they cried,

> "If our Master does not have mercy on us and forgive us, we will certainly be losers." [164]

Moses gathered around seventy leaders from all twelve tribes of Israelites and told them,

> "O my people! Surely you have wronged yourselves by worshiping the calf, so turn in repentance to your Creator and execute the calf worshippers among yourselves. That is best for you in the sight of your Creator." [165]

God commanded the Israelites to execute those among them who committed the calf worship. But they were doubtful about the God's command received from Moses and questioned its authenticity.

They said,

> "O Moses! We will never believe you until we see God with our own eyes," [166]

Crossing all the heights of arrogancy, to follow a command conveyed to them by their Prophet, they demanded to see God themselves and hear the command directly.

As a punishment from God for such an arrogant attitude, a thunderbolt struck them while they were looking on [166]. And all those seventy leaders died.

Moses cried,

> "My Master! Had You willed, You could have destroyed them long ago, and me as well,"

> "Will You destroy us for what the foolish among us have done?"

> "This is only a test from You - by which You allow whoever you will to stray and guide whoever You will,"

> "You are our Guardian. So forgive us and have mercy on us. You are the best forgiver." [167]

Not every one of the Israelites worshiped the idol of the golden calf, so Moses prayed to God not to punish all of them for the crime committed by some members.

God accepted the prayer of Moses and brought those leaders back to life [168]. After that Israelites obeyed the command of God and executed those who worshiped the idol of the golden calf.

ISRAELITES WERE CONTINUOUSLY DISOBEDIENT

Complaining about Food

Children of Israel complained to Moses about the food they had been blessed in that desert,

> "O Moses! We cannot endure the same meal every day. So just call upon your Master on our behalf, He will bring forth for us some of what the earth produces of herbs, cucumbers, garlic, lentils, and onions." [169]

Moses scolded them.

> "Do you exchange what is better for what is worse? You can go down to any village and you will find what you have asked for." [169]

Israelites felt bored eating the same food every day. In Egypt, they used to eat herbs, garlic, onions, cucumber, etc. But there in that desert, they got to eat Manna and Quails every day.

But they forgot that in Egypt, they might have had the option to eat a variety of food, but there they used to have an inhuman life, enslaved in ghettos and being tortured by the army. Even their newborn sons used to be killed by the Pharaoh every other year.

Instead of being grateful to God for granting them freedom from that life, they were complaining about the same food every day. They were not even grateful to receive food and water in that desert by which the whole nation of the Israelites was surviving; otherwise, they would have died of starvation and thrust into that extremely hot environment.

Delaying to follow the command of GOD

An Israeli man was murdered, but nobody knew who killed him; people were pointing fingers at each other, so much so that a civil war between the tribes was about to break out.

To avoid the chaos and civil war, the Israelites asked Moses to pray to God to inform them of the name of the killer. [170]

Moses said to his people,

"God commands you to sacrifice a cow."

They replied,

"Are you mocking us?" [171]

The reply showed how arrogant and ungrateful they were. After all the things they experienced, they still doubted the prophethood of Moses, as if he commanded them to do something from his own wish.

Moses responded,

"I seek refuge in God from acting foolishly!" [171]

When the Israelites realized that the command to sacrifice a cow was indeed from God,

They asked Moses,

"Call upon your Master to clarify for us what type of cow it should be!"

He replied,

"God says, 'The cow should neither be old nor young but in between. So do as you are commanded!'" [172]

But the Israelites did not have the intention to follow the command immediately.

They said,

"Call upon your Master to specify for us its color."

Moses replied,

"God says, it should be a bright yellow cow - pleasant to see.'" [173]

Again, they said,

> "Call upon your Master so that He may make clear to us which cow, for all cows look the same to us. Then, God willing, we will be guided to the right one." [174]

Moses replied,

> "God says, 'it should have been used neither to till the soil nor water the fields; wholesome and without blemish.'"

Israelites said,

> "Now you have come with the truth." Yet they still slaughtered it hesitantly! [175]

With all those unnecessary inquiries, the Israelites just made the job difficult for themself; they could have just sacrificed any cow at the very first instance of receiving the command from God.

After they sacrificed the cow, God instructed them to strike the dead body of the murdered person with a piece of meat from the cow. With that, God brought the dead body alive. [176]

The dead person became alive for an instance and told everyone present there, who killed him. After delivering the information, he died again. It was known that his own nephew was the killer.

Slandering about Moses

Moses was a shy person and used to cover his body completely because of his extensive shyness.

One of the children of Israel hurt him by saying,

"He covers his body in this way only because of some defect in his skin, either leprosy or scrotal hernia, or he has some other defect."

God wished to clear Moses of what they said about him, [177]

So, one day while Moses was in seclusion, he took off his clothes, put them on a stone, and started taking a bath. When he had finished the bath, he moved towards his clothes so as to take them, but the stone took his clothes and fled.

Moses picked up his stick and ran after the stone saying,

"O stone! Give me my garment!"

Till he reached a group of Israelites man who saw him naked and found him the best of what God had created. That was how God cleared him of what they had accused him of.

Mountain hovering above Israelites

Children of Israel were engaged in worshiping an idol of golden calf and they blamed the incident on one of their member, named Samiri. Then God revealed the Tablet Torah for them as a guideline for every aspect of life and told them that if they followed the commandments of the Torah firmly, they would be honored and blessed everywhere.

But they were continuously rebellious to the commandments mentioned in the Torah. They took everything for granted and had little fear of punishment from God.

They became so rebellious to the law of the Torah that as a warning, God raised a mountain above them. The Israelites were seeing the horrific sight of a mountain hovering above them and getting down to perish them to the earth.

To save themselves, they gave their covenant to hold firmly to the Torah and observe its teachings so they could become mindful of God." [178]

MOSES' JOURNEY WITH KHIDR

Once Moses stood up and addressed the children of Israel. He was asked who was the most learned man among the people. He said: "I." He believed so, as God had given him the power of miracles and honored him with the Torah. However, God revealed to Moses that no man could know all there is to know, nor would one messenger alone be the custodian of all knowledge. There would always be another who knew what others did not.

God said to him,

> "At the junction of the two seas, there is a slave of Mine who is more learned than you."

Moses said,

> "O my Master! How can I meet him?"

God said:

> "Take a fish and put it in a large basket and you will find him at the place where you will lose the fish."

With that aim, Moses said to his young assistant,

"I will never give up until I reach the junction of the two seas, even if I travel for ages." [179]

But when they finally reached the point where the seas met, they forgot their salted fish, and it made its way into the sea, slipping away wondrously. [180]

When they had passed further, he said to his assistant,

"Bring us our meal! We have certainly been exhausted by today's journey." [181]

He replied,

"Do you remember when we rested by the rock? That is when I forgot the fish. None made me forget to mention this except the devil. And the fish made its way into the sea miraculously." [182]

Moses responded,

"That is exactly what we were looking for."

So they returned, retracing their footsteps. [183]

There they saw a man lying covered with a garment [184]. Moses greeted him, and he replied saying,

"How do people greet each other in your land?"

Moses said,

"I am Moses."

The man asked,

> "Moses from Children of Israel?"

Moses said,

> "Yes, I have come to you so that you may teach me from those things which God has taught you."

He said,

> "O Moses! I have some of the knowledge which God has taught me and which you do not know, while you have some of the knowledge which God has taught you and which I do not know."

Moses asked,

> "May I follow you, provided that you teach me some of the right guidance you have been taught?" [185]

He said,

> "You certainly cannot be patient enough with me.[186]

> "And how can you be patient with what is beyond your realm of knowledge?" [187]

Moses assured him,

> "You will find me patient, God willing, and I will not disobey any of your orders." [188]

He responded,

> "Then if you follow me, do not question me about anything until I myself clarify it for you." [189]

> So both of them set out walking along the seashore. A boat passed by them, and they asked the crew of the boat to take them on board. The crew recognized the man; his name was Khidr, so they took them on board without fare.

> When they were on board the boat, a sparrow came and stood on the edge of the boat and dipped its beak once or twice into the sea.

Khidr said to Moses:

> "O Moses! My knowledge and your knowledge have not decreased God's knowledge except as much as this sparrow has decreased the water of the sea with its beak."

Then suddenly, Khidr took an axe and pulled up a plank from the boat,

Moses said to him:

> "What have you done? They took us on board charging us nothing, yet you have intentionally made a hole in their boat."

> "Have you done this to drown its people? You have certainly done a terrible thing!" [190]

He replied,

> "Did I not say that you cannot have patience with me?" [191]

Moses pleaded,

"Excuse me for forgetting, and do not be hard on me." [192]

So they proceeded until they came across a boy, and Khidr killed him.

Moses protested,

"Have you killed an innocent soul, who killed no one? You have certainly done a horrible thing." [193]

He answered,

"Did I not tell you that you cannot have patience with me?" [194]

Moses replied,

"If I ever question you about anything after this, then do not keep me in your company, for by then I would have given you enough of an excuse." [195]

So they moved on until they came to the people of a town. They asked them for food, but the people refused to give them hospitality. There they found a wall ready to collapse, so Khidr set it right.

Moses said,

"These are the people whom we have called on, but they neither gave us food, nor entertained us as guests, yet you have repaired their wall.

"If you wanted, you could have demanded a fee for this." [196]

Khidr replied,

"This is the parting of our ways. I will explain to you what you could not bear patiently. [197]

"As for the boat, it belonged to some poor people, working at sea. So I intended to damage it, for there was a tyrant king ahead of them who seizes every good ship by force." [198]

"And as for the boy, his parents were true believers, and we feared that he would pressure them into defiance and disbelief." [199]

"So we hoped that their Master would give them another, more virtuous and caring in his place." [200]

"And as for the wall, it belonged to two orphan boys in the city, and under the wall was a treasure that belonged to them, and their father had been a righteous man. So your Master willed that these children should come of age and retrieve their treasure, as a mercy from your Master."

"I did not do it all on my own. This is the explanation of what you could not bear patiently." [201]

ISRAELITES DISOBEY THE COMMAND TO ENTER JERUSALEM

Moses commanded the Israelites,

> "O my people! Enter the holy land which God has destined for you to enter. And do not turn back or else you will become losers." [202]

Moses conveyed the command of God to the Israelites to enter the city of present-day Jerusalem, where their father Prophet Israel used to live. In the bible prophet Israel was mentioned as Jacob. Later on he and his twelve sons along with their household, moved to Egypt during the time of Prophet Joseph.

During the time of the exodus of the Israelites from Egypt, a mighty strong nation was living in Jerusalem. So entering the city meant the Israelites had to fight with them.

Although Moses promised them victory, the Israelites refused to obey the command,

They replied,

> "O Moses! There is an enormously powerful people there, so we will never be able to enter it until they leave. If they do, then we will enter!" [203]

Moses sent a few leaders to spy out the city of Jerusalem. When they returned, two leaders among them suggested,

> "Surprise them through the gate. If you do, you will certainly prevail. Put your trust in God if you are truly believers." [204]

But the report made by the other leaders was so disappointing that the Israelites cried out in disgust and refused to march on.

They said,

> "O Moses! Still, we will never enter as long as they remain there. So go both you and your Master and fight; we are staying right here!" [205]

On a number of occasions, the Israelites already proved themselves as an ungrateful and arrogant nation.

God saved the Israelites from the oppression of Pharaoh, who used to kill their newborn sons, but immediately after getting freedom, they turned to worship an idol of a Golden calf.

God blessed them with Manna and Quail as food and water from rocks in that desert, but they demanded herbs and vegetables of Egypt days.

God blessed them with the revelation of the Torah as a guideline, but they were always arguing and delaying to follow the commandments unless forced by a mountain hovering over them.

After everything Moses did for them, they always doubted his message and even did not hesitate to spread slander about him.

So, characteristics like trusting and relying on God were not in that generation of Israelites' hearts.

For their disobedience, God cursed them,

> "Then this land is forbidden to them for forty years, during which they will wander through the land. So do not grieve for the rebellious people." [206]

For forty years the Israelites lived in that Sinai desert; every morning they went out to reach a city but by evening they just returned to the same place, the desert.

All the men except two who were in their 20s during the time of exodus died in that forty-year period; they never had the blessing to live in Jerusalem. After forty years in that desert, by the blessing of God, the new generation of Israelites conquered Jerusalem city under the leadership of Prophet Joshua.

DEATH OF PROPHET MOSES

After the Israelites refused to follow the command of God to enter the city of present-day Jerusalem,

Moses pleaded to God,

> "My Master! I have no control over anyone except myself and my brother. So set us apart from the rebellious people." [207]

Moses did not want to be with that rebellious nation anymore. God accepted his prayer. It is reported that Moses died few days after that incident.

He asked God that He bring him near the sacred land at a distance of a stone's throw. His wish was accepted, and the grave of Prophet Moses (peace be upon him) is by the way near the red sand hill.

STORY OF PROPHET JOSEPH

Prophet Israel (in the bible, his name is mentioned as Jacob) used to live in Canaan, encompassing the geographical area of present-day Palestine, Israel, Jordan, Lebanon, and Syria. So how did the children of Israel end up in Egypt in the first place? The answer lies in the story of Prophet Joseph.

Prophet Jacob had twelve sons; Joseph was the eleventh one. Benjamin the youngest and Joseph were from the same mother; the other ten were Joseph's half-brothers. Joseph was the most beloved son to Jacob, and for that, his half-brothers were very jealous of him.

Joseph, still a child woke up one day seeing a dream and told his father,

> "O my dear father! Indeed I dreamt of eleven stars, and the sun, and the moon, I saw them prostrating to me!" [208]

Jacob, himself a prophet, understood his son's dream was not like other ordinary dreams. It was a vision of the future. He also understood that his other sons would become more jealous and envious of Joseph if they knew about the dream.

So, he replied,

> "O my dear son! Do not relate your vision to your brothers, or they will devise a plot against you. [209]

He also advised him,

> "And so will your Master choose you, O Joseph, and teach you the interpretation of dreams, and perfect His favor upon you and the descendants of Jacob, just as He once perfected it upon your forefathers, Abraham and Isaac. Surely your Master is All-Knowing, All-Wise." [210]

Jacob was telling Joseph that in the past, God favored their forefathers, Prophet Abraham and Prophet Isaac, with other blessings. And from the sign of Joseph's dream, he also understood that God would choose Joseph as a prophet and favor him by granting him the ability to interpret dreams.

Somewhere else, the ten half-brothers of Joseph were discussing,

> "Surely Joseph and his brother Benjamin are more beloved to our father than we, even though we are a group of so many. Indeed, our father is clearly mistaken." [211]

The ten brothers used to move around as a group and they were proud of that, thinking how their father could not see that strength.

They were so envious of Joseph that they even discussed to kill him,

> "Kill Joseph or cast him out to some distant land so that our father's attention will be only ours, then after that you may repent and become righteous people!" [212]

One of them said,

> "Do not kill Joseph. But if you must do something, throw him into the bottom of a well so perhaps he may be picked up by some travelers." [213]

So, the brothers reached a plan to take Joseph with them in the name of an outdoor picnic and then throw him in a well. They went to their father for permission to take Joseph with them.

They said,

> "O our father! Why do you not trust us with Joseph, although we truly wish him well? [214]

> "Send him out with us tomorrow so that he may enjoy himself and play. And we will really watch over him." [215]

Jacob responded,

> "It would truly sadden me if you took him away with you, and I fear that a wolf may devour him while you are negligent of him." [216]

They said,

> "If a wolf were to devour him, despite our strong group, then we would certainly be losers!" [217]

The ten brothers took Joseph away and threw him into the bottom of the well as per their plan. [218]

Then they returned to their father in the evening, weeping. [219]

"Our father! We went racing and left Joseph with our belongings, and a wolf devoured him! But you will not believe us, no matter how truthful we are." [220]

As proof, they brought his shirt, stained with false blood. He responded,

"No! Your souls must have tempted you to do something evil. So I can only endure with beautiful patience! It is God's help that I seek to bear your claims." [221]

Jacob understood the half-brothers did something terrible with Joseph, but he had no other option except to rely on God and have patience.

There some travelers camped near the well and sent their water-boy who let down his bucket into the well.

He cried out,

"Oh, what a great find! Here is a boy!"

Joseph was surviving by holding a stone in the well; when the bucket was sent down for water, he grabbed the rope. The travelers took him secretly to be sold as merchandise, [222]

They later sold him for a cheap price, just a few silver coins, only wanting to get rid of him. [223]. The man who brought the child Joseph, was a minister of Egypt.

He took the child to his wife and said,

> "Take good care of him, perhaps he may be useful to us or we may adopt him as a son." [224]

The boy who was destined to be killed in that well, later on, sold as a slave, got a place to live in an Egyptian palace.

As a house of a minister, a lot of discussion regarding the kingdom's affairs used to occur there. As Joseph was growing up and working there as a slave, he might have heard those discussions while doing his daily work. By the time he became young and matured, he had gained much knowledge and wisdom from those insights. [225]

Joseph was a very good-looking man, and his noble character even made him more attracted to others. The lady, the wife of the minister, had some strong attraction towards Joseph. One day, she tried to seduce him.

She locked the doors firmly and said,

> "Come to me!"

But Joseph was a very loyal and noble character person.

He replied,

> "God is my refuge! It is not right to betray my master, who has taken good care of me. Indeed, the wrongdoers never succeed." [226]

Joseph reminded the lady that he could not betray her husband's trust, who gave him a place to live and eat. But She ignored his words and advanced towards him, [227] and to save himself from the situation,

Joseph ran towards the door to get out of the room. She ran behind him and tore his shirt from the back.

They find her husband at the door. Seeing him, she immediately tried to shift the blame to Joseph.

She cried,

"What is the penalty for someone who tried to violate your wife, except imprisonment or a painful punishment?" [228]

Joseph responded,

"It was she who tried to seduce me."

So, a witness from her own family testified,

"If his shirt is torn from the front, then she has told the truth and he is a liar. [229]

But if it is torn from the back, then she has lied and he is truthful." [230]

So, when her husband saw that Joseph's shirt was torn from the back,

He said to her,

"This must be an example of the cunning of you women! Indeed, your cunning is so shrewd!" [231]

Her husband understood the real scenario, but as a politician, he could not take any action against his wife, which might damage his political standing in the public.

So, he said,

"O Joseph! Forget about this."

"And you O wife! Seek forgiveness for your sin. It certainly has been your fault." [232]

But this type of incident in a palace finds a way to spread through gossip.

Some women of the city gossiped,

"The Chief Minister's wife is trying to seduce her slave-boy. Love for him has plagued her heart. Indeed, we see that she is clearly mistaken. [233]

The minister's wife became a laughingstock in her known circle. When she heard about their gossip, she invited them and set a banquet for them. She gave each one a knife, might to cut some particular dish on their plate, then said to Joseph,

"Come out before them."

When the ladies saw Joseph, they were so stunned by his beauty that they cut their hands with that knife with an absent mind, and exclaimed,

"Good God! This cannot be human; this must be a noble angel!" [234]

The minster's wife said to them,

"This is the one for whose love you criticized me! I did try to seduce him but he firmly refused. And if he does not do what I order him to, he will certainly be imprisoned and fully disgraced." [235]

The lady was so desperate, did not hesitate to threaten Joseph in front of the other ladies, who were equally attracted to him. To save himself from the sin of committing adultery,

Joseph prayed to God,

> "My Master! I would rather be in jail than do what they invite me to. And if You do not turn their cunning away from me, I might yield to them and fall into ignorance." [236]

So, despite all the proof of his innocence, he ended up in prison. [237]

Two other men went to jail with Joseph. Those two prisoners might realize Joseph was not like other prisoners in the jail and by interacting with him, they might also get some idea about the level of his knowledge and wisdom.

The two prisoners saw some ambiguous dreams, and for the interpretation, they went to Joseph.

One of them said,

> "I dreamt I was pressing wine."

The other said,

> "I dreamt I was carrying some bread on my head, from which birds were eating."

So, they both said,

> "Tell us their interpretation, for we surely see you as one of the good-doers." [238]

Joseph replied,

> "I can even tell you what kind of meal you will be served before you receive it. This knowledge is from what my Master has taught me. I have shunned the faith of a people who disbelieve in One God and deny the Hereafter." [239]

> "I follow the faith of my fathers: Abraham, Isaac, and Jacob. It is not right for us to associate anything with One God in worship. This is part of God's grace upon us and humanity, but most people are not grateful." [240]

> "O my fellow-prisoners! Which is far better: many different gods or God, the One, the Supreme?" [241]

> "Whatever idols you worship instead of Him are mere names which you and your forefathers have made up - a practice the One God has never authorized. It is only One God Who decides. He has commanded that you worship none but Him. That is the upright faith, but most people do not know." [242]

Joseph was in prison without committing any crime but even there, he was preaching the religion he was following, so that other prisoners could be guided to the right path of life. What a noble heart and character he had!

He then answered the interpretation of their dreams,

"O my fellow-prisoners! The first one of you will serve wine to his master, and the other will be crucified and the birds will eat from his head. The matter about which you inquired has been decided." [243]

Then he said to the one he knew would survive,

"Mention me in the presence of your master."

The interpretations became true; the prisoner who was freed got a job serving wine to the king. But he forgot to mention about Joseph to the King, so he remained in prison for several years. [244]

One day the King said,

"I dreamt of seven fat cows eaten up by seven skinny ones; and seven green ears of grain and seven others dry. O chiefs! Tell me the meaning of my dream if you can interpret dreams." [245]

They replied,

"These are confused visions and we do not know the interpretation of such dreams." [246]

Finally, the surviving ex-prisoner remembered Joseph after a long time and said,

"I will tell you it's interpretation, so send me forth to Joseph." [247]

He said,

> "Joseph, O man of truth! Interpret for us the dream of seven fat cows eaten up by seven skinny ones; and seven green ears of grain and seven others dry, so that I may return to the people and let them know." [248]

Joseph replied,
> "You will plant grain for seven consecutive years, leaving in the ear whatever you will harvest, except for the little you will eat." [249]

> "Then after that will come seven years of great hardship which will consume whatever you have saved, except the little you will store for seed." [250]

> "Then after that will come a year in which people will receive abundant rain and they will press oil and wine." [251]

After hearing the interpretation, The King then said,

> "Bring him to me."

When the messenger from the king came, Joseph requested to initiate an inquiry about his imprisonment; he declined to quit the prison till his character was cleared.

> "Go back to your master and ask him about the case of the women who cut their hands." [252]

Those women were gathered in the royal court and

The King asked them,

"What did you get when you tried to seduce Joseph?"

They replied,

"God forbids! We know nothing indecent about him."
Then the Chief Minister's wife admitted,

"Now the truth has come to light. It was I who tried to seduce him, and he is surely truthful. [253]

"From this, Joseph should know that I did not speak dishonestly about him in his absence." [254]

"And I do not seek to free myself from blame, for indeed the soul is ever inclined to evil, except those shown mercy by my Master, surely my Master is All-Forgiving, Most Merciful." [255]

King understood Joseph was innocent and also realized that the person who could interpret a dream like that should possess excellent knowledge and wisdom.

So, The King commanded,

"Bring him to me. I will employ him exclusively in my service."

And when Joseph spoke to him, the King said,

"Today you are highly esteemed and fully trusted by us." [256]

Joseph proposed,

> "Put me in charge of the store-houses of the land, for I am truly reliable and adept." [257]

The king agreed and Joseph was appointed as the minister in charge of treasury.

From prison to the finance minister of the kingdom! This is how God established Joseph in the land to settle wherever he pleased. He never discounts the reward of the good-doers. [258]

After seven years of good harvest, when the phase of famine started, the Economy of Egypt was not impacted due to diligent management by Joseph but other surrounding countries were not prepared at all. People of those regions were facing severe hardship. They used to travel to Egypt to sell their goods in return for getting some grain. Each man used to get one camel load of grains. Joseph's brothers also from their home in Canaan traveled to Egypt with that same goal.

When they came and entered in Joseph's presence, he recognized them but they were unaware of who he really was. [259]

When he had provided them with their supplies, the ten brothers requested one extra camel load of grains for their youngest half-brother left at home.

Joseph agreed but demanded,

> "Bring me your brother on your father's side. Do you not see that I give full measure and I am the best of hosts? [260]

He asked them to bring their youngest brother next year as proof. Also cautioned them that without him, they would not get any grain at all.

"But if you do not bring him to me next time, I will have no grain for you, nor will you ever come close to me again." [261]

They promised,

"We will try to convince his father to let him come. We will certainly do our best." [262]

Joseph ordered his servants to put his brothers' money back into their saddlebags so that they would find it when they returned to their family and perhaps, they would come back. [263]

When Joseph's brothers returned to their father, they pleaded,

"O our father! We have been denied further supplies. So send our brother with us so that we may receive our measure, and we will definitely watch over him." [264]

He responded,

"Should I trust you with him as I once trusted you with his brother Joseph?" [265]

When they opened their bags, they discovered that their money had been returned to them. They argued,

"O our father! What more can we ask for? Here is our money, fully returned to us. Now we can buy more food for our family. We will watch over our brother, and obtain an extra camel-load of grain. That load can be easily secured." [266]

Jacob insisted,

> "I will not send him with you until you give me a solemn oath by God that you will certainly bring him back to me unless you are totally overpowered."

Then after they had given him their oaths, he concluded,

> "God is a Witness to what we have said." [267]

He then instructed them,

> "O my sons! Do not enter the city all through one gate but through separate gates. I cannot help you against what is destined by God in the least. It is only God Who decides. In Him, I put my trust. And in Him let the faithful put their trust." [268]

He cautioned his sons that they should not move together with all those grains, which might prompt others to robbery. When they entered Joseph's presence, he called his brother Benjamin aside, and confided to him,

> "I am indeed your brother Joseph! So do not feel distressed about what they have been doing." [269]

Joseph wanted to keep his younger brother Benjamin with him and made a plan for that. When Joseph had provided them with supplies, he asked a maid to slip the royal cup into his brother's bag.

Then a herald cried,

> "O people of the caravan! You must be thieves!" [270]

They asked, turning back,

"What have you lost?" [271]

The herald along with the guards replied,

"We have lost the King's measuring cup. And whoever brings it will be awarded a camel-load of grain. I guarantee it." [272]

Joseph's brothers replied,

"By God! You know well that we did not come to cause trouble in the land, nor are we thieves." [273]

Joseph's men asked,

"What should be the price for theft, if you are lying?" [274]

Joseph's brothers responded,

"The price will be the enslavement of the one in whose bag the cup is found. That is how we punish the wrongdoers." [275]

Joseph's servant began searching their bags before that of his brother Benjamin, then brought it out of Benjamin's bag. [276]

To distance themselves, Joseph's brothers argued,

"If he has stolen, so did his full brother before."

Hearing that lie about himself, Joseph was outraged but suppressed it, revealing nothing to them, and said to himself,

"You are in such an evil position, and God knows best the truth of what you claim." [277]

They appealed,

"O Chief Minister! He has a very old father, so take one of us instead. We surely see you as one of the good-doers." [278]

Joseph responded,

"God forbid that we should take other than the one with whom we found our property. Otherwise, we would surely be unjust." [279]

When they lost all hope in him and left, on the way back they spoke privately.

The eldest of them said,

"Do you not know that your father had taken a solemn oath by God from you, nor how you failed him regarding Joseph before? So I am not leaving this land until my father allows me to, or God decides for me. For He is the Best of Judges. [280]

After returning home, they said to Jacob,

"O our father! Your son committed theft. We testify only to what we know. We could not guard against the unforeseen." [281]

"Ask the people of the land where we were and the caravan we traveled with. We are certainly telling the truth." [282]

He cried,

"No! Your souls must have tempted you to do something evil. So I am left with nothing but beautiful patience! I trust God will return them all to me. Surely, He alone is the All-Knowing, All-Wise." [283]

After so many years, Jacob still had the hope that God would return Joseph along with Benjamin to him.

He turned away from them, lamenting,

"Alas, poor Joseph!"

And his eyes turned white out of the grief he suppressed. [284]

Separation from Joseph was so painful for Jacob that after crying for all those years, he became blind.

His other children were criticizing him,

"By God! You will not cease to remember Joseph until you lose your health or even your life." [285]

He replied,

"I complain of my anguish and sorrow only to God, and I know from God what you do not know. [286]

O my sons! Go and search diligently for Joseph and his brother. And do not lose hope in the mercy of God, for no one loses hope in God's mercy except those with no faith." [287]

Next year they again traveled to Egypt for new supplies, and when they entered Joseph's presence,

They pleaded,

> "O Chief Minister! We and our family have been touched with hardship, and we have brought only a few worthless coins, but please give us our supplies in full and be charitable to us. Indeed, God rewards the charitable." [288]

This time Joseph planned to make things straight with his half-brothers,

He asked them,

> "Do you remember what you did to Joseph and his brother in your ignorance?" [289]

They replied in shock,

> "Are you really Joseph?"

He said,

> "I am Joseph, and here is my brother Benjamin! God has truly been gracious to us. Surely whoever is mindful of God and patient, then certainly God never discounts the reward of the good-doers." [290]

They admitted,

> "By God! God has truly preferred you over us, and we have surely been sinful." [291]

Joseph forgave them and said,

> "There is no blame on you today. May God forgive you! He is the Most Merciful of the merciful! [292]

He then gave one of his shirts to them and said,

> "Go with this shirt of mine and cast it over my father's face, and he will regain his sight. Then come back to me with your whole family." [293]

There in Canaan, Jacob might sense something in his mind; when the caravan departed from Egypt, he said to those around him,

> "You may think I am senile, but I certainly sense the smell of Joseph." [294]

They replied,

> "By God! You are definitely still in your old delusion." [295]

But when the bearer of the good news arrived, he cast the shirt over Jacob's face so he regained his sight.

Jacob then said to his children,

> "Did I not tell you that I truly know from God what you do not know?" [296]

They begged,

> "O our father! Pray for the forgiveness of our sins. We have certainly been sinful." [297]

He said,

> "I will pray to my Master for your forgiveness. He alone is indeed the All-Forgiving, Most Merciful." [298]

> Jacob and all his sons with their households, left Canaan for Egypt. When they entered Joseph's presence, he received his parents graciously and said,

> "Enter Egypt, God willing, in security." [299]

Joseph was the chief minister of Egypt then, so he assured his family members that they could live in Egypt without any kind of fear.

Then he raised his parents to the throne, and they all fell down in prostration to Joseph,

Who then said,

> "O my dear father! This is the interpretation of my old dream. My Master has made it come true. He was truly kind to me when He freed me from prison and brought you all from the desert after the devil had ignited rivalry between me and my siblings. Indeed my Master is subtle in fulfilling what He wills. Surely He alone is the All-Knowing, All-Wise." [300]

He prayed to God,

> "My Master! You have surely granted me authority and taught me the interpretation of dreams. O Originator of the heavens and the earth! You are my Guardian in this world and the Hereafter. Allow me to die as one who submits and join me with the righteous." [301]

***This was how all the Children of Israel migrated from Canaan to Egypt.**

Out of extreme jealousy, ten half-brothers threw Joseph into a well, who ended up in an Egyptian palace as a slave. At a young age, he was imprisoned for a number of years despite being innocent. There he helped two fellow prisoners to interpret their dreams, which eventually paved the way for him to be the minister of the treasury of that kingdom.

Fast forward a number of years, his half-brothers traveled all the way to Egypt, desperately in need of food during that period of famine. Eventually, prophet Joseph (peace be upon him) forgave his brothers and asked them all to migrate to Egypt along with their parents to have a safe, secure, and honorable life.

But they did not know just after a century what miserable life was waiting for their future generation under a new Pharaoh, from where the story of the prophet Moses (peace be upon him) begins.

REFLECTION AND LEARNINGS

1. Pharaonic characteristics are still present in the society.

We may hate the Pharaoh, but instead of hating him, we should hate the characteristics of Pharaoh and be aware of whether those are present in us?

Oppression by dividing a society

The Pharaoh used to rule Egypt by dividing the society into different classes. He bestowed privileges and preferential rights on some to make them the ruling class and reduced others to oppression and exploitation.

In that society, the Israelites were the subject of oppression and exploitation. They were forced to do all sorts of mean and hard work for the Coptic people, who were the ruling class.

This type of scenario is still seen in our present world, where society is divided by race, ethnicity, or culture, and the minority is oppressed by the ruling class.

Emotional blackmail

After coming from exile, when Moses confronted the Pharaoh in his royal court, instead of admitting the oppression to the Israelites, Pharaoh tried to emotionally blackmail Moses. He reminded Moses that he adopted and raised him in his palace.

We, ordinary humans, also often use the same tactics to avoid a logical argument. With those tactics, we try to divert the primary point of argument but may not understand that those tactics may cause severe consequences in someone else's life.

By hearing some legitimate complaints of abuse from the employees, the employer, instead of addressing the complaint, reminds them how ungrateful they were to have a job to survive.

It was just an example; similar scenarios can be found in many other cases of present society, in personal life, family life, professional life, political culture, etc. By practicing this type of tactic, we are just imitating the Pharaoh.

Imposing guilty consciousness

When Pharaoh failed to divert the argument by emotional blackmail, he tried to impose guilty consciousness on Moses by reminding him that he had killed a man.

Similarly, instead of concentrating on the legitimate point raised by a person, we often try to undermine it by pointing out flaws in the person's history. The primary aim of that tactic is to silence that voice.

Misleading the fact

Moses asked the Pharaoh to release the Israelites from slavery and allow them to go with him. But Pharaoh was telling his nation that Moses was planning to overthrow the government and rule the Copts; the oppressor was trying to paint themselves as the future victim.

Height of oppression

To keep his kingship, the Pharaoh was killing newborn children, and that was not a one-time case; the utterly barbaric act continued for many years.

In our present world, in the name of economic growth, some corporations and governments are practicing unethical activities like polluting the environment through excessive carbon emission, chemical waste in the water, arms selling to conflict zones, selling violent video games which affects mental health, etc. Pharaoh was killing babies for the greed of power, and we are destroying the future of our children for the greed of wealth.

2. Rely on God and do your best in every situation.

Mother and Sister of Moses

When God inspired Moses' mother to cast the baby into the river in a basket, she did that by relying on God, but after that she did not sit idly; she asked her daughter to follow the basket. In that situation, that's the best she could do to ensure her newborn son's safety.

And the sister of Moses, she did her best to follow her mother's command. She totally understood the consequences if the spies or soldiers of the Pharaoh found her brother in the basket, so she followed him as such that others' attention did not divert to the floating basket.

When the baby Moses was picked from the blank at the Palace of Pharaoh, his sister was wandering outside, to know the fate of her brother. She did not panic or create a scene. When the opportunity arrived, she introduced her mother as a wet nurse to the royal maids, resulting in the baby Moses reuniting with his mother.

Moses and his stick

A stick turned into a giant snake was a divine sign granted by God, but Moses did not rely on that stick only. He confronted the Pharaoh in his royal court and won the arguments with him by logic and a clear message, defying all the diversion tactics from the Pharaoh. Moses did not use the stick at the very first moment of entering the royal court to frighten the Pharaoh and ministers to get their attention.

He participated in the showdown with the topmost magicians of the kingdom, where the Pharaoh and the entire kingdom were on one side, and only Moses and his brother were on the other.

For ten years, Pharaoh was trying to kill Moses, but that did not frighten Moses; he was doing his work of preaching as best he could and relying on God for his own and the Israelites' safety. He could have used the stick-turned snake to save himself in every situation, but not once did he use the power of the stick without the permission of God.

Joseph in the Prison

Even though Joseph was innocent, he ended up in prison. But there, he did not remain idle and relied only on God to get out from there.

He earned respect from fellow prisoners by noble manners and wise talking. God blessed him with the knowledge of interpreting dreams. He used that knowledge to help those two prisoners and requested the person who would become free to mention about him to his master. Eventually, due to that help, Joseph got out of prison after a few years.

Steps taken by Joseph to address the famine

By interpreting the king's dream, Joseph warned everyone about the famine, but he did not stop there. When he saw the opportunity, he asked for the post of treasury.

He took all the necessary steps to address the famine. Due to his skill and strategic management of the crops grown in the first seven years, the kingdom was able to address the famine of the next seven years.

3. Use the position to do good.

Moses as a Prince

The Pharaoh adopted Moses, so he was growing up as the prince of Egypt, but that status did not prevent him from doing good for others. At his young age, Moses used to go out to help others in the middle of the day when the outside temperature used to be so hot that everyone stayed home.

Joseph as a Minister

By interpreting the king's dream, Joseph got his freedom from prison, regained his honor as a noble person, and got the position of Minister. He could have lived a lavish life, but he chose the treasury post. Managed the crisis of famine to save the kingdom and its citizens.

When his half-brothers arrived in his court for help, instead of taking revenge, he not only gave them grain and other supplies but eventually helped them to settle in Egypt.

4. A simple good act can change a lot in life.

Very often, we think about doing something big. We plan big with much planning and analysis and expect something impactful from those big actions. But we forget that sometimes a small but genuine good act can also impact a lot in life.

Moses helping the girls

When Moses reached Midian, he was mentally and physically exhausted, but that did not prevent him from helping those two girls struggling to water their herds.

It was a simple good act by him, and most of us may not expect much from that. But for that small good act, Moses got a place to live, a job to survive, and most importantly, he got a family. Moses got everything a man needs in life by that small kind act.

Joseph helping the fellow prisoners

Joseph helped his two fellow prisoners by interpreting their dreams. That simple help not only facilitated Joseph to get out of prison but also cleared his name from all the false blame and even made him the Minister of the treasury of the kingdom.

5. Truth always prevails.

Moses confronting the Pharaoh

Pharaoh was the most powerful king of that era and Moses was an ordinary man in fact a fugitive, when he confronted the Pharaoh in his royal court. So naturally, Moses was supposed to be afraid to talk in front of the Pharaoh. But from the conversation between them, it is seen Moses was the one speaking with authority because the truth was on his side.

Truth gives the courage to confront anyone, even a tyrant like the Pharaoh.

Magicians' submission to God

Pharaoh and his ministers thought the signs Moses showed them in the royal court were magic. So, they gathered a team of magicians from all over the kingdom to defeat Moses in a competition.

When the competition started and magicians saw that their magic had just been swallowed within a second by the stick-turned snake of Moses, they fell to prostration to God.

At that moment, those magicians did not see anything but the truth. They did not see the Pharaoh; they did not see the crowd; all they saw was a true sign of God in front of them.

That truth has given them so much courage and strength in mind that they were ready to bear the horrific torture the Pharoah was threatening them, and eventually ready to sacrifice their life.

Innocence of Joseph

When the minister caught his wife and Joseph in a closed room, the lady tried to shift the blame of adultery to Joseph. But by the advice of their family friend, when they found that Joseph's shirt was torn at the back, everybody understood Joseph was innocent.

Even when the king inquired about the case of Joseph, who was in prison for a number of years, all the ladies confessed to the king that Joseph was innocent of the crime he was accused of.

6. Signs and Magic are not the same.

Everything in this world is a sign from God. Sky and other things in the sky, like galaxies, stars, planets, etc, all are signs from God. Similarly, the water, earth, trees, and humans; the list is just endless.

But things that are always in front of our eyes often seem very ordinary to us. We don't give that much attention to those.

So, sometimes God showed some new signs humans had not experienced or witnessed before. He showed those signs as a warning or as a blessing for the people.

Some people or nations confused those signs as magic or could not distinguish between these two. Magic is an illusion, and it never sustains. It has limitations, but a Sign from God does not.

A stick turned into a giant snake was a sign for the Pharaoh and his people. They denied it at the first incident, but when their hand-picked top magicians also confirmed it as a sign from God, they rejected that just for pure arrogance.

Locusts, lice, and water-like blood all over the place in Egypt were not magic; those were warning signs from God for the Coptic people.

Parting of water to make a path in the sea was not magic; God chose to rescue the Israelites in this way so that by seeing this sign, they understood the magnitude of God's power and were grateful to Him.

Torah revealed as a written tablet was another great sign, which God blessed upon the Israelites.

A mountain hovering above the Israelites was not magic; it was a reality to them and, in fact was a warning from God for disobeying the law of Torah.

7. Fate and Wisdom

Fate is something beyond our understanding, and there are some wisdoms behind the fate which only God knows. From the journey of Moses with Khidr, we get some idea about those wisdoms.

The life of Prophet Joseph can be a good example of Fate and Wisdom also. His brothers threw him in a well. At that moment, most of us might think of that incident as a terrible fate for Joseph.

Things did not stop there. After being separated from his beloved father, Joseph became a slave in Egypt and ended up in prison at a young age. Things were just getting worse for him. But he never lost his faith in God. Even in prison, he was preaching about the favor of God.

One day the king saw a dream, and by interpreting that dream, Joseph got the chance to get the post of a Minister. He gained prominence in the kingdom by skillfully managing the famine years. Eventually, his family also reunited with him in Egypt.

What a turn of fate. Only God can plan this.

8. People like Samiri are still present in society.

Samiri was the master planner of worshiping the golden calf in the absence of Moses. He initiated and indulged the Israelites in this. He even convinced them by saying that the Golden Calf was the lost God of Moses.

The fearful thing for us is that people like Samiri are still present in the society. The primary tactic they use is mixing falsehood with the truth.

For the vast majority of the people in society, religion is an emotional thing only and people like Samiri play with that emotion; they study the religious scripture, take some provisions from there, and then mix it with their own falsehood. When someone challenges them, they give a very ambiguous explanation.

Sometimes, they even discourage people from reading the Scripture, with the argument that not all are capable of understanding it. Then they try to impose their view or interpretations on others. Very often they do this for economic benefit or to gain influence in society.

To save ourselves from these Samiris, the first thing we have to do is to read the Scripture and use our intellect to understand and analyze the words, God has revealed for us as guidance. We can go and ask someone knowledgeable for better understanding, but we should not follow them blindly.

9. Never violate the favors of God

In this world, God blessed us with so many favors, and he has also granted us superior intellect than his other creations. But he warns us not to abuse that position of superiority by saying,

> "Eat from (use) the good things We have provided for you, but do not transgress in them, or My wrath will befall you. And whoever My wrath befalls is certainly doomed." [302]

The context of this verse is about the time when God blessed the Israelites with food like Manna and Quail in the Sinai desert.

Everyone in this world loves to have knowledge, health, wealth, and honor in society. God commanded us to work hard for these provisions by using the intellect and guidance he has blessed us. But the real test begins when we get these blessings. If we become grateful to God for those blessings and use those for the betterment of family, neighbors, society, and nation, then more good will happen everywhere, but if we transgress and misuse those blessings by being unjust to others and causing corruption in the society, then God's wrath will befall on us.

By studying the history of the rise and fall of the nations, we can find out how truthful this verse is.

REFERENCES

[1]   Chapter 28, Verse 04 of the Quran

Indeed, Pharaoh arrogantly elevated himself in the land and divided its people into subservient groups, one of which he persecuted, slaughtering their sons and keeping their women. He was truly one of the corruptors.

[2]   Chapter 28, Verse 07 of the Quran

We inspired the mother of Moses: "Suckle him, but when you fear for him, cast him into the river, and do not fear or grieve. We will certainly return him to you, and make him one of the messengers."

[3]   Chapter 28, Verse 11 of the Quran

And she said to his sister, "Keep track of him!" So she watched him from a distance, while they were unaware.

[4]   Chapter 28, Verse 09 of the Quran

Pharaoh's wife said to him, "This baby is a source of joy for me and you. Do not kill him. Perhaps he may be useful to us or we may adopt him as a son." They were unaware of what was to come.

[5]   Chapter 28, Verse 12 of the Quran

And We had caused him to refuse all wet nurses at first, so his sister suggested, "Shall I direct you to a family who will bring him up for you and take good care of him?"

[6]   Chapter 28, Verse 13 of the Quran

This is how We returned him to his mother so that her heart would be put at ease, and not grieve, and that she would know that Allah's promise is always true. But most people do not know.

[7]   Chapter 28, Verse 14 of the Quran

And when he reached full strength and maturity, We gave him wisdom and knowledge. This is how We reward the good-doers.

[8]   Chapter 28, Verse 15 of the Quran

One day he entered the city unnoticed by its people. There he found two men fighting: one of his own people, and the other of his enemies. The man from his people called to him for help against his foe. So Moses punched him, causing his death. Moses cried, "This is from Satan's handiwork. He is certainly a sworn, misleading enemy."

[9]   Chapter 28, Verse 16 of the Quran

He pleaded, "My Master! I have definitely wronged my soul, so forgive me." So He forgave him, for He is indeed the All-Forgiving, Most Merciful.

[10]   Chapter 28, Verse 18 of the Quran
And so Moses became fearful, watching out in the city, when
suddenly the one who sought his help the day before cried out to
him again for help. Moses rebuked him, "Indeed, you are clearly a
troublemaker."

[11]   Chapter 28, Verse 19 of the Quran

Then when Moses was about to lay his hands on their foe, the
enemy said, "O Moses! Do you intend to kill me as you killed a
man yesterday? You only want to be a tyrant in the land. You do
not intend to make peace!"

[12]   Chapter 28, Verse 20 of the Quran

And there came a man, rushing from the farthest end of the city. He
said, "O Moses! The chiefs are actually conspiring against you to
put you to death, so leave the city. I really advise you to do so."

[13]   Chapter 28, Verse 21 of the Quran

So Moses left the city in a state of fear and caution, praying, "My
Master! Deliver me from the wrongdoing people."

[14]   Chapter 28, Verse 22 of the Quran

And as he made his way towards Midian, he said, "I trust my Lord
will guide me to the right way."

[15]   Chapter 28, Verse 23 of the Quran

When he arrived at the well of Midian, he found a group of people
watering their herds. Apart from them, he noticed two women

holding back their herd'. He asked them, "What is the problem?" They replied, "We cannot water our animals until the other shepherds are done, for our father is a very old man."

[16]   Chapter 28, Verse 24 of the Quran

So he watered their herd for them, then withdrew to the shade and prayed, "My Master! I am truly in desperate need of whatever provision You may have in store for me."

[17]   Chapter 28, Verse 25 of the Quran

Then one of the two women came to him, walking bashfully. She said, "My father is inviting you so he may reward you for watering our animals for us." When Moses came to him and told him his whole story, the old man said, "Have no fear! You are now safe from the wrongdoing people."

[18]   Chapter 28, Verse 26 of the Quran

One of the two daughters suggested, "O my dear father! Hire him. A strong, trustworthy person is definitely the best to hire."

[19]   Chapter 28, Verse 27 of the Quran

The old man proposed, "I wish to marry one of these two daughters of mine to you, provided that you stay in my service for eight years. If you complete ten, it will be a favor from you, but I do not wish to make it difficult for you. Allah willing, you will find me an agreeable man."

[20]   Chapter 28, Verse 28 of the Quran

Moses responded, "Then it is settled between you and I. Whichever term I fulfill, there will be no further obligation on me. And Allah is a Witness to what we say."

[21]   Chapter 28, Verse 29 of the Quran

When Moses had completed the term and was traveling with his family, he spotted a fire on the side of Mount Tur. He said to his family, "Stay here, for I have spotted a fire. Perhaps from there, I can bring you some directions or a torch from the fire so you may warm yourselves."

[22]   Chapter 20, Verse 10 of the Quran

When he saw a fire, he said to his family, "Wait here, for I have spotted a fire. Perhaps I can bring you a torch from it, or find some guidance at the fire."

[23]   Chapter 28, Verse 30 of the Quran

But when he came to it, he was called from the bush in the sacred ground to the right side of the valley: "O Moses! It is truly I. I am Allah—the Lord of all worlds."

[24]   Chapter 20, Verse 12 of the Quran

It is truly I. I am your Lord! So take off your sandals, for you are in the sacred valley of Tuwa.

[25]   Chapter 20, Verse 13 of the Quran

I have chosen you, so listen to what is revealed.

[26]   Chapter 20, Verse 14 of the Quran

'It is truly I. I am Allah! There is no god worthy of worship except Me. So worship Me alone, and establish prayer for My remembrance.

[27]   Chapter 20, Verse 15 of the Quran

The Hour is sure to come. My Will is to keep it hidden, so that every soul may be rewarded according to their efforts.

[28]   Chapter 20, Verse 16 of the Quran

So do not let those who disbelieve in it and follow their desires distract you from it, or you will be doomed."

[29]   Chapter 20, Verse 17 of the Quran

Allah added, "And what is that in your right hand, O Moses?"

[30]   Chapter 20, Verse 18 of the Quran

He replied, "It is my staff! I lean on it, and with it, I beat down branches for my sheep and have other uses for it."

[31]   Chapter 20, Verse 19 of the Quran

Allah said, "Throw it down, O Moses!"

[32]   Chapter 20, Verse 20 of the Quran

So he did, then — behold! — it became a serpent, slithering.

[33]   Chapter 28, Verse 31 of the Quran

Now, throw down your staff!" But when he saw it slithering like a snake, he ran away without looking back. Allah reassured him, "O Moses! Draw near, and have no fear. You are perfectly secure."

[34]   Chapter 20, Verse 21 of the Quran

Allah said, "Take it and have no fear. We will return it to its former state.

[35]   Chapter 20, Verse 22 of the Quran

And put your hand under your armpit; it will come out shining white, unblemished, as another sign.

[36]   Chapter 20, Verse 23 of the Quran

So that We may show you some of Our greatest signs.

[37]   Chapter 28, Verse 32 of the Quran

Now, put your hand through the opening of your collar; it will come out shining white, unblemished. And cross your arms tightly to calm your fears. These are two proofs from your Lord to Pharaoh and his chiefs. They have truly been a rebellious people."

[38]   Chapter 26, Verse 12 of the Quran

He replied, "My Lord! I fear that they will reject me.

[39]   Chapter 28, Verse 33 of the Quran

Moses appealed, "My Master! I have indeed killed a man from them, so I fear they may kill me."

[40]   Chapter 28, Verse 34 of the Quran

"And my brother Aaron is more eloquent than I, so send him with me as a helper to support what I say, for I truly fear they may reject me."

[41]   Chapter 28, Verse 35 of the Quran

Allah responded, "We will assist you with your brother and grant you both authority, so they cannot harm you. With Our signs, you and those who follow you will certainly prevail."

[42]   Chapter 20, Verse 25 of the Quran

Moses prayed, "My Lord! Uplift my heart for me,

[43]   Chapter 20, Verse 26 of the Quran

And make my task easy,

[44]   Chapter 20, Verse 27 of the Quran

And remove the impediment from my tongue.

[45]   Chapter 20, Verse 28 of the Quran

So people may understand my speech,

[46]   Chapter 20, Verse 36 of the Quran

Allah responded, "All that you requested has been granted, O Moses!

[47]   Chapter 20, Verse 37 of the Quran

And surely, We had shown you favour before,

[48]   Chapter 20, Verse 38 of the Quran

When We inspired your mother with this:

[49]   Chapter 20, Verse 39 of the Quran

Put him into a chest, then put it into the river. The river will wash it ashore, and he will be taken by Pharaoh, an enemy of Mine and his. And I endeared you with love from Me, O Moses, so that you would be brought up under My watchful Eye.

[50]   Chapter 20, Verse 40 of the Quran

Remember, when your sister came along and proposed, 'Shall I direct you to someone who will nurse him?' So We reunited you with your mother so that her heart would be put at ease, and she would not grieve. Later you killed a man by mistake, but We saved you from sorrow, as well as other tests We put you through. Then you stayed for a number of years among the people of Midian. Then you came here as pre-destined, O Moses!

[51] Chapter 20, Verse 41 of the Quran

And I have selected you for My service.

[52] Chapter 20, Verse 47 of the Quran

So go to him and say, 'Indeed we are both messengers from your Lord, so let the Children of Israel go with us, and do not oppress them. We have come to you with a sign from your Master. And salvation will be for whoever follows the right guidance.

[53] Chapter 20, Verse 48 of the Quran

It has indeed been revealed to us that the punishment will be upon whoever denies the truth and turns away."

[54] Chapter 20, Verse 44 of the Quran

Speak to him gently, so perhaps he may be mindful of Me or fearful of My punishment.

[55]   Chapter 26, Verse 18 of the Quran

Pharaoh protested, "Did we not raise you among us as a child, and you stayed several years of your life in our care?

[56] Chapter 26, Verse 22 of the Quran

How can that be a favour, of which you remind me, when it was only because you have enslaved the Children of Israel?"

[57]   Chapter 26, Verse 19 of the Quran

Then you did what you did, being utterly ungrateful.

[58]   Chapter 26, Verse 20 of the Quran

Moses replied, "I did it then, lacking guidance.

[59]   Chapter 26, Verse 21 of the Quran

So I fled from you when I feared you. Then my Lord granted me wisdom and made me one of the messengers.

[60]   Chapter 20, Verse 49 of the Quran

Pharaoh asked, "Who then is the Master of you two, O Moses?"

[61]   Chapter 26, Verse 23 of the Quran

Pharaoh asked, "And what is the Master of all dominions?

[62]   Chapter 20, Verse 50 of the Quran

He answered, "Our Master is the One Who has given everything its distinctive form, then guided it."

[63]   Chapter 26, Verse 24 of the Quran

Moses replied, "He is the Master of the heavens and the earth and everything in between, if only you had sure faith."

[64]   Chapter 26, Verse 25 of the Quran

Pharaoh said to those around him, "Did you hear what he said?"

[65]   Chapter 26, Verse 26 of the Quran

Moses added, "He is your Master and the Master of your forefathers."

[66]   Chapter 26, Verse 27 of the Quran

Pharaoh said mockingly, "Indeed, your messenger, who has been sent to you, is insane."

[67]   Chapter 26, Verse 28 of the Quran

Moses responded, "He is the Master of the east and west, and everything in between, if only you had any sense."

[68]   Chapter 20, Verse 53 of the Quran

He is the One Who has laid out the earth for all of you, and set in it pathways for you, and sends down rain from the sky, causing various types of plants to grow

[69]   Chapter 28, Verse 38 of the Quran

Pharaoh declared, "O chiefs! I know of no other god for you but myself. So bake bricks out of clay for me, O Haman, and build a high tower so I may look at the God of Moses, although I am sure he is a liar."

[70]   Chapter 26, Verse 29 of the Quran

Pharaoh threatened, "If you take any other god besides me, I will certainly have you imprisoned."

[71]   Chapter 26, Verse 30 of the Quran

Moses responded, "Even if I bring you a clear proof?"

[72]   Chapter 26, Verse 31 of the Quran
Pharaoh demanded, "Bring it then if what you say is true."

[73]   Chapter 26, Verse 32 of the Quran

So he threw down his staff and - behold! — it became a real snake.

[74]   Chapter 26, Verse 33 of the Quran

Then he drew his hand out of his collar and it was shining white for all to see.

[75]   Chapter 26, Verse 34 of the Quran

Pharaoh said to the chiefs around him, "He is indeed a skilled magician,

[76]   Chapter 26, Verse 35 of the Quran

who seeks to drive you from your land by his magic. So what do you propose?"

[77]   Chapter 26, Verse 36 of the Quran

They replied, "Let him and his brother wait and dispatch mobilizers to all cities

[78]   Chapter 26, Verse 37 of the Quran

to bring you every skilled magician.

[79]   Chapter 20, Verse 58 of the Quran

We can surely meet you with similar magic. So set for us an appointment that neither of us will fail to keep, in a central place.

[80]   Chapter 20, Verse 59 of the Quran

Moses said, "Your appointment is on the Day of the Festival, and let the people be gathered mid-morning."

[81]   Chapter 26, Verse 39 of the Quran

And the people were asked, "Will you join the gathering?

[82]   Chapter 26, Verse 40 of the Quran

so that we may follow the magicians if they prevail."

[83]   Chapter 26, Verse 41 of the Quran

When the magicians came, they asked Pharaoh, "Shall we have a suitable reward if we prevail?"

[84]   Chapter 26, Verse 42 of the Quran

He replied, "Yes, and you will then certainly be among those closest to me."

[85]   Chapter 20, Verse 61 of the Quran

Moses warned the magicians, "Woe to you! Do not fabricate a lie against Allah, or He will wipe you out with a torment. Whoever fabricates ˹lies˺ is bound to fail."

[86]   Chapter 20, Verse 62 of the Quran
So the magicians disputed the matter among themselves, conversing privately.

[87]   Chapter 20, Verse 63 of the Quran

They concluded, "These two are only magicians who want to drive you out of your land with their magic and do away with your most cherished traditions.

[88]   Chapter 20, Verse 65 of the Quran

They said, "O Moses! Either you throw, or let us be the first to throw."

[89]   Chapter 20, Verse 66 of the Quran

"No, you go first." And suddenly their ropes and staffs seemed to him from their magic that they were moving like snakes.

[90]   Chapter 20, Verse 67 of the Quran

So, Moses concealed fear within himself.

[91]   Chapter 20, Verse 68 of the Quran

We reassured him, "Do not fear! It is certainly you who will prevail.

[92]   Chapter 20, Verse 69 of the Quran

Cast what is in your right hand, and it will swallow up what they have made, for what they have made is no more than a magic trick. And magicians can never succeed wherever they go.

[93]   Chapter 26, Verse 45 of the Quran

Then Moses threw down his staff, and at once it devoured the objects of their illusion!

[94]   Chapter 26, Verse 46 of the Quran

So the magicians fell down, prostrating.

[95]   Chapter 26, Verse 47 of the Quran

They declared, "We now believe in the Master of all dominion."

[96]   Chapter 26, Verse 48 of the Quran

"The Master of Moses and Aaron."

[97]   Chapter 26, Verse 49 of the Quran

Pharaoh threatened, "How dare you believe in him before I give
you permission? He must be your master who taught you magic,
but soon you will see. I will certainly cut off your hands and feet on
opposite sides, then crucify you all."

[98]   Chapter 20, Verse 72 of the Quran

They responded, "By the One Who created us! We will never
prefer you over the clear proofs that have come to us. So do
whatever you want! Your authority only covers the worldly life."

[99]   Chapter 20, Verse 73 of the Quran

Indeed, we have believed in our Lord so He may forgive our sins
and that magic you have forced us to practice. And Allah is far
superior in reward and more lasting in punishment."

[100]   Chapter 07, Verse 127 of the Quran

The chiefs of Pharaoh's people protested, "Are you going to leave
Moses and his people free to spread corruption in the land and
abandon you and your gods?" He responded, "We will kill their
sons and keep their women. We will completely dominate them."

[101]   Chapter 40, Verse 25 of the Quran

Then, when he came to them with the truth from Us, they said,
"Kill the sons of those who believe with him and keep their
women." But the plotting of the disbelievers was only in vain.

[102]   Chapter 40, Verse 26 of the Quran

And Pharaoh said, "Let me kill Moses, and let him call upon his Lord! I truly fear that he may change your traditions or cause mischief in the land."

[103]   Chapter 40, Verse 28 of the Quran

A believing man from Pharaoh's people, who was hiding his faith, argued, "Will you kill a man only for saying: 'My Master is Allah,' while he has in fact come to you with clear proofs from your Master? If he is a liar, it will be to his own loss. But if he is truthful, then you will be afflicted with some of what he is threatening you with. Surely Allah does not guide whoever is a transgressor, a total liar.

[104]   Chapter 40, Verse 29 of the Quran

O my people! Authority belongs to you today, reigning supreme in the land. But who would help us against the torment of Allah, if it were to befall us?" Pharaoh assured his people, "I am telling you only what I believe, and I am leading you only to the way of guidance."

[105]   Chapter 40, Verse 30 of the Quran

And the man who believed cautioned, "O my people! I truly fear for you the doom of earlier enemy forces

[106]   Chapter 40, Verse 31 of the Quran

like the fate of the people of Noah, 'Âd, Thamûd, and those after them. For Allah would never will to wrong His servants.

[107]   Chapter 40, Verse 32 of the Quran

O my people! I truly fear for you the Day all will be crying out to each other

[108]   Chapter 40, Verse 33 of the Quran

the Day you will try in vain to turn your backs and run away, with no one to protect you from Allah. And whoever Allah leaves to stray will be left with no guide.

[109]   Chapter 40, Verse 34 of the Quran

Joseph already came to you earlier with clear proofs, yet you never ceased to doubt what he came to you with. When he died you said, 'Allah will never send a messenger after him.' This is how Allah leaves every transgressor and doubter to stray

[110]   Chapter 40, Verse 38 of the Quran

And the man who believed urged, "O my people! Follow me, and I will lead you to the Way of Guidance.

[111]   Chapter 40, Verse 39 of the Quran

O my people! This worldly life is only a fleeting enjoyment, whereas the Hereafter is truly the home of settlement.

[112]   Chapter 40, Verse 41 of the Quran

O my people! How is it that I invite you to salvation, while you invite me to the Fire!

[113] Chapter 40, Verse 42 of the Quran

You invite me to disbelieve in Allah and associate with Him what I have no knowledge of, while I invite you to the Almighty, Most Forgiving.

[114] Chapter 40, Verse 43 of the Quran

There is no doubt that whatever idols you invite me to worship are not worthy to be invoked either in this world or the Hereafter. Undoubtedly, our return is to Allah, and the transgressors will be the inmates of the Fire.

[115] Chapter 40, Verse 44 of the Quran

You will remember what I say to you, and I entrust my affairs to Allah. Surely Allah is All-Seeing of all His servants."

[116] Chapter 07, Verse 128 of the Quran

Moses reassured his people, "Seek Allah's help and be patient. Indeed, the earth belongs to Allah alone. He grants it to whoever He chooses of His servants. The ultimate outcome belongs only to the righteous."

[117] Chapter 07, Verse 129 of the Quran

They complained, "We have always been oppressed — before and after you came to us with the message." He replied, "Perhaps your Lord will destroy your enemy and make you successors in the land to see what you will do."

[118]   Chapter 07, Verse 130 of the Quran

Indeed, We afflicted Pharaoh's people with famine and shortage of crops so they might come back to their senses.

[119]   Chapter 07, Verse 133 of the Quran

So We plagued them with floods, locusts, lice, frogs, and blood all as clear signs, but they persisted in arrogance and were a wicked people.

[120]   Chapter 07, Verse 131 of the Quran

In times of prosperity, they said, "This is what we deserve," but in adversity, they blamed it on Moses and those with him. Surely all is destined by Allah. Yet most of them did not know.

[121]   Chapter 07, Verse 132 of the Quran

They said, "No matter what sign you may bring to deceive us, we will never believe in you."

[122]   Chapter 07, Verse 134 of the Quran

When tormented, they pleaded, "O Moses! Pray to your Lord on our behalf, by virtue of the covenant He made with you. If you help remove this torment from us, we will certainly believe in you and let the Children of Israel go with you."

[123]   Chapter 07, Verse 135 of the Quran

But as soon as We removed the torment from them—until they met their inevitable fate—they broke their promise.

[124]   Chapter 26, Verse 52 of the Quran

And We inspired Moses, saying, "Leave with My servants at night, for you will surely be pursued."

[125]   Chapter 26, Verse 53 of the Quran

Then Pharaoh sent mobilizers to all cities,

[126]   Chapter 26, Verse 54 of the Quran

and said, "These outcasts are just a handful of people",

[127]   Chapter 26, Verse 55 of the Quran

who have really enraged us,

[128]   Chapter 26, Verse 56 of the Quran

but we are all on the alert.

[129]   Chapter 26, Verse 60 of the Quran

And so they pursued them at sunrise

[130]   Chapter 26, Verse 61 of the Quran

When the two groups came face to face, the companions of Moses cried out, "We are overtaken for sure.

[131]   Chapter 26, Verse 62 of the Quran

Moses reassured them, "Absolutely not! My Master is certainly with me — He will guide me.

[132]   Chapter 26, Verse 63 of the Quran

So We inspired Moses: "Strike the sea with your staff," and the sea was split; each part was like a huge mountain.

[133]   Chapter 26, Verse 64 of the Quran

We drew the pursuers to that place

[134]   Chapter 26, Verse 65 of the Quran

and delivered Moses and those with him all together.

[135]   Chapter 26, Verse 66 of the Quran

Then We drowned the others.

[136]   Chapter 07, Verse 137 of the Quran

We made the people who had been oppressed to inherit the eastern regions of the land and the western ones, which we had blessed. And the word of your master was fulfilled for the children of Israel because of what they patiently endured. And we destroyed all that Pharaoh and his people constructed and what they established

[137]   Chapter 07, Verse 138 of the Quran

We brought the Children of Israel across the sea and they came upon a people devoted to idols. They demanded, "O Moses! Make for us a god like their gods." He replied, "Indeed, you are a people acting ignorantly!

[138]   Chapter 07, Verse 139 of the Quran

What they follow is certainly doomed to destruction and their deeds are in vain."

[139]   Chapter 07, Verse 140 of the Quran

He added, "Shall I seek for you a god other than Allah, while He has honored you above the others?"

[140]   Chapter 07, Verse 160 of the Quran

We divided them into twelve tribes — each as a community. And We revealed to Moses, when his people asked for water, "Strike the rock with your staff." Then twelve springs gushed out. Each tribe knew its drinking place. We shaded them with clouds and sent down to them manna and quails, saying, "Eat from the good things We have provided for you." They certainly did not wrong Us, but wronged themselves.

[141]   Chapter 07, Verse 142 of the Quran

We appointed for Moses thirty nights then added another ten — completing his Lord's term of forty nights. Moses commanded his brother Aaron, "Take my place among my people, do what is right, and do not follow the way of the corruptors."

[142]   Chapter 20, Verse 83 of the Quran

O Moses, what has made you come in haste from your people?

[143]   Chapter 20, Verse 84 of the Quran

He replied, "They are close on my tracks. And I have hastened to
You, my Master, so You will be pleased."

[144]   Chapter 20, Verse 85 of the Quran

Allah responded, "We have indeed tested your people in your
absence, and the Saimiri has led them astray."

[145]   Chapter 07, Verse 143 of the Quran

When Moses came at the appointed time and his Master spoke to
him, he asked, "My Master! Reveal Yourself to me so I may see
You." Allah answered, "You cannot see Me! But look at the
mountain. If it remains firm in its place, only then will you see
Me." When his Master appeared to the mountain, He leveled it to
dust and Moses collapsed unconscious. When he recovered, he
cried, "Glory be to You! I turn to You in repentance and I am the
first of the believers."

[146]   Chapter 07, Verse 144 of the Quran

Allah said, "O Moses! I have already elevated you above all others
by My messages and speech So hold firmly to what I have given
you and be grateful."

[147]   Chapter 07, Verse 145 of the Quran

We wrote for him on the Tablets the fundamentals of everything; commandments and explanations of all things. We commanded, "Hold to this firmly and ask your people to take the best of it. I will soon show all of you the home of the rebellious.

[148]   Chapter 07, Verse 148 of the Quran

In the absence of Moses, his people made from their golden jewelry an idol of a calf that made a lowing sound. Did they not see that it could neither speak to them nor guide them to the right Path? Still, they took it as a god and were wrongdoers.

[149]   Chapter 20, Verse 90 of the Quran

Aaron had already warned them beforehand, "O my people! You are only being tested by this, for indeed your one true Master is the Most Compassionate. So follow me and obey my orders."

[150]   Chapter 20, Verse 91 of the Quran

They replied, "We will not cease to worship it until Moses returns to us."

[151]   Chapter 20, Verse 86 of the Quran

Then Moses returned to his people, furious and sorrowed, he said "O my people! Had your Master not made you a good promise? Has my absence been too long for you? Or have you wished for wrath from your Master to befall you, so you broke your promise to me?"

[152] Chapter 20, Verse 87 of the Quran

They argued, "We did not break our promise to you of our own free will, but we were made to carry the burden of the people's golden jewelry, then we threw it into the fire, and so did the Sâmiri."

[153] Chapter 20, Verse 88 of the Quran

Then he molded for them an idol of a calf that made a lowing sound. They said, "This is your god and the god of Moses, but Moses forgot where it was!"

[154] Chapter 07, Verse 150 of the Quran

When Moses returned to his people, totally furious and sorrowful, he said, "What an evil thing you committed in my absence! Did you want to hasten your Master's torment?" Then he threw down the Tablets and grabbed his brother by the hair, dragging him closer. Aaron pleaded, "O son of my mother! The people overpowered me and were about to kill me. So do not humiliate me and make my enemies rejoice, nor count me among the wrongdoing people."

[155] Chapter 20, Verse 92 of the Quran

Moses scolded his brother, "O Aaron! What prevented you, when you saw them going astray,

[156] Chapter 20, Verse 93 of the Quran

from following after me? How could you disobey my orders?"

[157]   Chapter 20, Verse 94 of the Quran

Aaron pleaded, "O son of my mother! Do not seize me by my beard or the hair of my head. I really feared that you would say, 'You have caused division among the Children of Israel, and did not observe my word."

[158]   Chapter 20, Verse 95 of the Quran

Moses then asked, "What did you think you were doing, O Sâmiri?"

[159]   Chapter 20, Verse 96 of the Quran

He said, "I saw what they did not see, so I took a handful of dust from the hoof-prints of the horse of the messenger-angel Gabriel then cast it on the molded calf. This is what my lower self tempted me into."

[160]   Chapter 20, Verse 97 of the Quran

Moses said, "Go away then! And for the rest of your life, you will surely be crying, 'Do not touch ˹me˺!' Then you will certainly have a fate that you cannot escape. Now look at your god to which you have been devoted: we will burn it up, then scatter it in the sea completely."

[161]   Chapter 20, Verse 98 of the Quran

Then Moses addressed his people, "Your only god is Allah; there is no god worthy of worship except Him. He encompasses everything in His knowledge."

[162]   Chapter 07, Verse 151 of the Quran

Moses prayed, "My Master! Forgive me and my brother! And admit us into Your mercy. You are the Most Merciful of the merciful."

[163]   Chapter 07, Verse 154 of the Quran

When Moses' anger subsided, he took up the Tablets whose text contained guidance and mercy for those who stand in awe of their Master.

[164]   Chapter 07, Verse 149 of the Quran

Later, when they were filled with remorse and realized they had gone astray, they cried, "If our Master does not have mercy on us and forgive us, we will certainly be losers."

[165]   Chapter 02, Verse 54 of the Quran

And remember when Moses said to his people, "O my people! Surely you have wronged yourselves by worshipping the calf, so turn in repentance to your Creator and execute the calf-worshippers among yourselves. That is best for you in the sight of your Creator." Then He accepted your repentance. Surely He is the Accepter of Repentance, Most Merciful.

[166]   Chapter 02, Verse 55 of the Quran

And remember when you said, "O Moses! We will never believe you until we see Allah with our own eyes," so a thunderbolt struck you while you were looking on.

[167]   Chapter 07, Verse 155 of the Quran

Moses chose seventy men from among his people for Our
appointment and, when they were seized by an earthquake, he
cried, "My Master! Had You willed, You could have destroyed
them long ago, and me as well. Will You destroy us for what the
foolish among us have done? This is only a test from You — by
which You allow whoever you will to stray and guide whoever You
will. You are our Guardian. So forgive us and have mercy on us.
You are the best forgiver.

[168]   Chapter 02, Verse 56 of the Quran

Then We brought you back to life after your death so that perhaps
you would be grateful.

[169]   Chapter 02, Verse 61 of the Quran

And remember when you said, "O Moses! We cannot endure the
same meal every day. So just call upon your Master on our behalf,
He will bring forth for us some of what the earth produces of herbs,
cucumbers, garlic, lentils, and onions." Moses scolded them, "Do
you exchange what is better for what is worse? You can go down to
any village and you will find what you have asked for." They were
stricken with disgrace and misery, and they invited the displeasure
of Allah for rejecting Allah's signs and unjustly killing the
prophets. This is a fair reward' for their disobedience and
violations.

[170]   Chapter 02, Verse 72 of the Quran

This is when a man was killed and you disputed who the killer was,
but Allah revealed what you concealed.

[171]   Chapter 02, Verse 67 of the Quran

And remember when Moses said to his people, "Allah commands you to sacrifice a cow." They replied, "Are you mocking us?" Moses responded, "I seek refuge in Allah from acting foolishly!"

[172]   Chapter 02, Verse 68 of the Quran

They said, "Call upon your Master to clarify for us what type of cow it should be!" He replied, "Allah says, 'The cow should neither be old nor young but in between. So do as you are commanded!'"

[173]   Chapter 02, Verse 69 of the Quran

They said, "Call upon your Master to specify for us its colour." He replied, "Allah says, 'It should be a bright yellow cow—pleasant to see.'"

[174]   Chapter 02, Verse 70 of the Quran

Again they said, "Call upon your Master so that He may make clear to us which cow, for all cows look the same to us. Then, Allah willing, we will be guided to the right one."

[175]   Chapter 02, Verse 71 of the Quran

He replied, "Allah says, 'It should have been used neither to till the soil nor water the fields; wholesome and without blemish.'" They said, "Now you have come with the truth." Yet they still slaughtered it hesitantly!

[176]   Chapter 02, Verse 73 of the Quran

So We instructed, "Strike the dead body with a piece of the cow."
This is how easily Allah brings the dead to life, showing you His
signs so that you may understand.

[177]   Chapter 33, Verse 69 of the Quran

O believers! Do not be like those who slandered Moses, but Allah
cleared him of what they said. And he was honorable in the sight of
Allah.

[178]   Chapter 02, Verse 63 of the Quran

And remember when We took a covenant from you and raised the
mountain above you saying, "Hold firmly to that Scripture which
We have given you and observe its teachings so perhaps you will
become mindful of Allah."

[179]   Chapter 18, Verse 60 of the Quran

And remember when Moses said to his young assistant, "I will
never give up until I reach the junction of the two seas, even if I
travel for ages."

[180]   Chapter 18, Verse 61 of the Quran

But when they finally reached the point where the seas met, they
forgot their salted fish, and it made its way into the sea, slipping
away wondrously.

[181]   Chapter 18, Verse 62 of the Quran

When they had passed further, he said to his assistant, "Bring us our meal! We have certainly been exhausted by today's journey."

[182]   Chapter 18, Verse 63 of the Quran

He replied, "Do you remember when we rested by the rock? That is when I forgot the fish. None made me forget to mention this except Satan. And the fish made its way into the sea miraculously."

[183]   Chapter 18, Verse 64 of the Quran

Moses responded, "That is exactly what we were looking for." So they returned, retracing their footsteps.

[184]   Chapter 18, Verse 65 of the Quran

There they found a servant of Ours, to whom We had granted mercy from Us and enlightened with knowledge of Our Own.

[185]   Chapter 18, Verse 66 of the Quran

Moses said to him, "May I follow you, provided that you teach me some of the right guidance you have been taught?"

[186]   Chapter 18, Verse 67 of the Quran

He said, "You certainly cannot be patient enough with me.

[187]   Chapter 18, Verse 68 of the Quran

And how can you be patient with what is beyond your realm of knowledge?"

[188]   Chapter 18, Verse 69 of the Quran

Moses assured him, "You will find me patient, Allah willing, and I will not disobey any of your orders."

[189]   Chapter 18, Verse 70 of the Quran

He responded, "Then if you follow me, do not question me about anything until I myself clarify it for you."

[190]   Chapter 18, Verse 71 of the Quran

So they set out, but after they had boarded a ship, the man made a hole in it. Moses protested, "Have you done this to drown its people? You have certainly done a terrible thing!"

[191]   Chapter 18, Verse 72 of the Quran

He replied, "Did I not say that you cannot have patience with me?"

[192]   Chapter 18, Verse 73 of the Quran

Moses pleaded, "Excuse me for forgetting, and do not be hard on me."

[193]   Chapter 18, Verse 74 of the Quran

So they proceeded until they came across a boy, and the man killed him. Moses protested, "Have you killed an innocent soul, who killed no one? You have certainly done a horrible thing."

[194]   Chapter 18, Verse 75 of the Quran

He answered, "Did I not tell you that you cannot have patience with me?"

[195]   Chapter 18, Verse 76 of the Quran

Moses replied, "If I ever question you about anything after this, then do not keep me in your company, for by then I would have given you enough of an excuse."

[196]   Chapter 18, Verse 77 of the Quran

So they moved on until they came to the people of a town. They asked them for food, but the people refused to give them hospitality. There they found a wall ready to collapse, so the man set it right. Moses protested, "If you wanted, you could have demanded a fee for this."

[197]   Chapter 18, Verse 78 of the Quran

He replied, "This is the parting of our ways. I will explain to you what you could not bear patiently.

[198]   Chapter 18, Verse 79 of the Quran

"As for the ship, it belonged to some poor people, working at sea. So I intended to damage it, for there was a ˹tyrant˺ king ahead of them who seizes every good ship by force.

[199]   Chapter 18, Verse 80 of the Quran

"And as for the boy, his parents were true believers, and we feared that he would pressure them into defiance and disbelief.

[200]   Chapter 18, Verse 81 of the Quran

So we hoped that their Lord would give them another, more virtuous and caring in his place.

[201]   Chapter 18, Verse 82 of the Quran

"And as for the wall, it belonged to two orphan boys in the city, and under the wall was a treasure that belonged to them, and their father had been a righteous man. So your Lord willed that these children should come of age and retrieve their treasure, as a mercy from your Lord. I did not do it all on my own. This is the explanation of what you could not bear patiently."

[202]   Chapter 05, Verse 21 of the Quran

"O my people! Enter the Holy Land, which Allah has destined for you to enter. And do not turn back, or else you will become losers."

[203] Chapter 05, Verse 22 of the Quran

They replied, "O Moses! There is an enormously powerful people there, so we will never be able to enter it until they leave. If they do, then we will enter!"

[204] Chapter 05, Verse 23 of the Quran

Two God-fearing men—who had been blessed by Allah—said, "Surprise them through the gate. If you do, you will certainly prevail. Put your trust in Allah if you are truly believers."

[205] Chapter 05, Verse 24 of the Quran

Yet they said, "O Moses! Still we will never enter as long as they remain there. So go—both you and your Lord—and fight; we are staying right here!"

[206] Chapter 05, Verse 26 of the Quran

Allah replied, "Then this land is forbidden to them for forty years, during which they will wander through the land. So do not grieve for the rebellious people."

[207] Chapter 05, Verse 25 of the Quran

Moses pleaded, "My Master! I have no control over anyone except myself and my brother. So set us apart from the rebellious people."

[208]   Chapter 12, Verse 04 of the Quran

Remember when Joseph said to his father, "O my dear father! Indeed I dreamt of eleven stars, and the sun, and the moon. I saw them prostrating to me!"

[209]   Chapter 12, Verse 05 of the Quran

He replied, "O my dear son! Do not relate your vision to your brothers, or they will devise a plot against you. Surely Satan is a sworn enemy to humankind.

[210]   Chapter 12, Verse 06 of the Quran

And so will your Master choose you O Joseph, and teach you the interpretation of dreams, and perfect His favour upon you and the descendants of Jacob — just as He once perfected it upon your forefathers, Abraham and Isaac. Surely your Lord is All-Knowing, All-Wise."

[211]   Chapter 12, Verse 08 of the Quran

Remember when they said to one another, "Surely Joseph and his brother Benjamin are more beloved to our father than we, even though we are a group of so many. Indeed, our father is clearly mistaken.

[212]   Chapter 12, Verse 09 of the Quran

Kill Joseph or cast him out to some distant land so that our father's attention will be only ours, then after that you may repent and become righteous people!"

[213]   Chapter 12, Verse 10 of the Quran

One of them said, "Do not kill Joseph. But if you must do
something, throw him into the bottom of a well so perhaps he may
be picked up by some travelers."

[214]   Chapter 12, Verse 11 of the Quran

They said, "O our father! Why do you not trust us with Joseph,
although we truly wish him well?

[215]   Chapter 12, Verse 12 of the Quran

Send him out with us tomorrow so that he may enjoy himself and
play. And we will really watch over him."

[216]   Chapter 12, Verse 13 of the Quran

He responded, "It would truly sadden me if you took him away
with you, and I fear that a wolf may devour him while you are
negligent of him."

[217]   Chapter 12, Verse 14 of the Quran

They said, "If a wolf were to devour him, despite our strong group,
then we would certainly be losers!"

[218]   Chapter 12, Verse 15 of the Quran

And so, when they took him away and decided to throw him into
the bottom of the well, We inspired him: "One day you will remind
them of this deed of theirs while they are unaware of who you are."

[219]   Chapter 12, Verse 16 of the Quran
Then they returned to their father in the evening, weeping.

[220]   Chapter 12, Verse 17 of the Quran

They cried, "Our father! We went racing and left Joseph with our belongings, and a wolf devoured him! But you will not believe us, no matter how truthful we are."

[221]   Chapter 12, Verse 18 of the Quran

And they brought his shirt, stained with false blood. He responded, "No! Your souls must have tempted you to do something evil. So I can only endure with beautiful patience! It is Allah's help that I seek to bear your claims."

[222]   Chapter 12, Verse 19 of the Quran

And there came some travelers, and they sent their water-boy who let down his bucket into the well. He cried out, "Oh, what a great find! Here is a boy!" And they took him secretly to be sold as merchandise, but Allah is All-Knowing of what they did.

[223]   Chapter 12, Verse 20 of the Quran

They later sold him for a cheap price, just a few silver coins only wanting to get rid of him.

[224]   Chapter 12, Verse 21 of the Quran

The man from Egypt who bought him said to his wife, "Take good care of him, perhaps he may be useful to us or we may adopt him as a son." This is how We established Joseph in the land, so that We might teach him the interpretation of dreams. Allah's Will always prevails, but most people do not know.

[225]   Chapter 12, Verse 22 of the Quran

And when he reached maturity, We gave him wisdom and knowledge. This is how We reward the good-doers.

[226]   Chapter 12, Verse 23 of the Quran

And the lady, in whose house he lived, tried to seduce him. She locked the doors firmly and said, "Come to me!" He replied, "Allah is my refuge! It is not right to betray my master, who has taken good care of me. Indeed, the wrongdoers never succeed."

[227]   Chapter 12, Verse 24 of the Quran

She advanced towards him, and he would have done likewise, had he not seen a sign from his Master. This is how We kept evil and indecency away from him, for he was truly one of Our chosen servants.

[228]   Chapter 12, Verse 25 of the Quran

They raced for the door and she tore his shirt from the back, only to find her husband at the door. She cried, "What is the penalty for someone who tried to violate your wife, except imprisonment or a painful punishment?"

[229]   Chapter 12, Verse 26 of the Quran

Joseph responded, "It was she who tried to seduce me." And a
witness from her own family testified: "If his shirt is torn from the
front, then she has told the truth and he is a liar.

[230]   Chapter 12, Verse 27 of the Quran

But if it is torn from the back, then she has lied and he is truthful."

[231]   Chapter 12, Verse 28 of the Quran

So when her husband saw that Joseph's shirt was torn from the
back, he said to her, "This must be an example of the cunning of
you women! Indeed, your cunning is so shrewd!

[232]   Chapter 12, Verse 29 of the Quran

O Joseph! Forget about this. And you O wife! Seek forgiveness for
your sin. It certainly has been your fault."

[233]   Chapter 12, Verse 30 of the Quran

Some women of the city gossiped, "The Chief Minister's wife is
trying to seduce her slave boy. Love for him has plagued her heart.
Indeed, we see that she is clearly mistaken."

[234]   Chapter 12, Verse 31 of the Quran

When she heard about their gossip, she invited them and set a
banquet for them. She gave each one a knife, then said to Joseph,
"Come out before them." When they saw him, they were so

stunned by his beauty that they cut their hands, and exclaimed, "Good God! This cannot be human; this must be a noble angel!"

[235]   Chapter 12, Verse 32 of the Quran

She said, "This is the one for whose love you criticized me! I did try to seduce him but he ˹firmly˺ refused. And if he does not do what I order him to, he will certainly be imprisoned and fully disgraced."

[236]   Chapter 12, Verse 33 of the Quran

Joseph prayed, "My Master! I would rather be in jail than do what they invite me to. And if You do not turn their cunning away from me, I might yield to them and fall into ignorance."

[237]   Chapter 12, Verse 35 of the Quran

And so it occurred to those in charge, despite seeing all the proofs of his innocence, that he should be imprisoned for a while.

[238]   Chapter 12, Verse 36 of the Quran

And two other servants went to jail with Joseph. One of them said, "I dreamt I was pressing wine." The other said, "I dreamt I was carrying some bread on my head, from which birds were eating." Then both said, "Tell us their interpretation, for we surely see you as one of the good-doers."

[239]   Chapter 12, Verse 37 of the Quran

Joseph replied, "I can even tell you what kind of meal you will be served before you receive it. This knowledge is from what my

Master has taught me. I have shunned the faith of a people who disbelieve in Allah and deny the Hereafter.

[240]   Chapter 12, Verse 38 of the Quran

I follow the faith of my fathers: Abraham, Isaac, and Jacob. It is not right for us to associate anything with Allah in worship. This is part of Allah's grace upon us and humanity, but most people are not grateful.

[241]   Chapter 12, Verse 39 of the Quran

O my fellow prisoners! Which is far better: many different lords or Allah — the One, the Supreme?

[242]   Chapter 12, Verse 40 of the Quran

Whatever idols you worship instead of Him are mere names which you and your forefathers have made up — a practice Allah has never authorized. It is only Allah Who decides. He has commanded that you worship none but Him. That is the upright faith, but most people do not know.

[243]   Chapter 12, Verse 41 of the Quran

"O my fellow-prisoners! The first one of you will serve wine to his master, and the other will be crucified and the birds will eat from his head. The matter about which you inquired has been decided."

[244]   Chapter 12, Verse 42 of the Quran

Then he said to the one he knew would survive, "Mention me in the presence of your master." But Satan made him forget to mention Joseph to his master, so he remained in prison for several years.

[245]   Chapter 12, Verse 43 of the Quran

And one day the King said, "I dreamt of seven fat cows eaten up by seven skinny ones; and seven green ears of grain and seven others dry. O chiefs! Tell me the meaning of my dream if you can interpret dreams."

[246]   Chapter 12, Verse 44 of the Quran

They replied, "These are confused visions and we do not know the interpretation of such dreams."

[247]   Chapter 12, Verse 45 of the Quran

Finally, the surviving ex-prisoner remembered Joseph after a long time and said, "I will tell you its interpretation, so send me forth to Joseph."

[248]   Chapter 12, Verse 46 of the Quran

He said, "Joseph, O man of truth! Interpret for us the dream of seven fat cows eaten up by seven skinny ones; and seven green ears of grain and seven others dry, so that I may return to the people and let them know."

[249]   Chapter 12, Verse 47 of the Quran

Joseph replied, "You will plant grain for seven consecutive years, leaving in the ear whatever you will harvest, except for the little you will eat.

[250]   Chapter 12, Verse 48 of the Quran

Then after that will come seven years of great hardship which will consume whatever you have saved, except the little you will store for seed.

[251]   Chapter 12, Verse 49 of the Quran

Then after that will come a year in which people will receive abundant rain and they will press oil and wine."

[252]   Chapter 12, Verse 50 of the Quran

The King then said, "Bring him to me." When the messenger came to him, Joseph said, "Go back to your master and ask him about the case of the women who cut their hands. Surely my Lord has full knowledge of their cunning."

[253]   Chapter 12, Verse 51 of the Quran

The King asked the women, "What did you get when you tried to seduce Joseph?" They replied, "Allah forbid! We know nothing indecent about him." Then the Chief Minister's wife admitted, "Now the truth has come to light. It was I who tried to seduce him, and he is surely truthful.

[254]   Chapter 12, Verse 52 of the Quran

From this, Joseph should know that I did not speak dishonestly about him in his absence, for Allah certainly does not guide the scheming of the dishonest.

[255]   Chapter 12, Verse 53 of the Quran

And I do not seek to free myself from blame, for indeed the soul is ever inclined to evil, except those shown mercy by my Lord. Surely my Lord is All-Forgiving, Most Merciful."

[256]   Chapter 12, Verse 54 of the Quran

The King said, "Bring him to me. I will employ him exclusively in my service." And when Joseph spoke to him, the King said, "Today you are highly esteemed and fully trusted by us."

[257]   Chapter 12, Verse 55 of the Quran

Joseph proposed, "Put me in charge of the store-houses of the land, for I am truly reliable and adept."

[258]   Chapter 12, Verse 56 of the Quran

This is how We established Joseph in the land to settle wherever he pleased. We shower Our mercy on whoever We will, and We never discount the reward of the good-doers.

[259]   Chapter 12, Verse 58 of the Quran

And Joseph's brothers came and entered his presence. He recognized them but they were unaware of who he really was.

[260]   Chapter 12, Verse 59 of the Quran

When he had provided them with their supplies, he demanded, "Bring me your brother on your father's side. Do you not see that I give full measure and I am the best of hosts?

[261]   Chapter 12, Verse 60 of the Quran

But if you do not bring him to me next time, I will have no grain for you, nor will you ever come close to me again."

[262]   Chapter 12, Verse 61 of the Quran

They promised, "We will try to convince his father to let him come. We will certainly do our best."

[263]   Chapter 12, Verse 62 of the Quran

Joseph ordered his servants to put his brothers' money back into their saddlebags so that they would find it when they returned to their family and perhaps they would come back.

[264]   Chapter 12, Verse 63 of the Quran

When Joseph's brothers returned to their father, they pleaded, "O our father! We have been denied further supplies. So send our brother with us so that we may receive our measure, and we will definitely watch over him."

[265]   Chapter 12, Verse 64 of the Quran

He responded, "Should I trust you with him as I once trusted you with his brother Joseph? But only Allah is the best Protector, and He is the Most Merciful of the merciful."

[266]   Chapter 12, Verse 65 of the Quran

When they opened their bags, they discovered that their money had been returned to them. They argued, "O our father! What more can we ask for? Here is our money, fully returned to us. Now we can buy more food for our family. We will watch over our brother, and obtain an extra camel-load of grain. That load can be easily secured."

[267]   Chapter 12, Verse 66 of the Quran

Jacob insisted, "I will not send him with you until you give me a solemn oath by Allah that you will certainly bring him back to me, unless you are totally overpowered." Then after they had given him their oaths, he concluded, "Allah is a Witness to what we have said."

[268]   Chapter 12, Verse 67 of the Quran

He then instructed them, "O my sons! Do not enter the city all through one gate but through separate gates. I cannot help you against what is destined by Allah in the least. It is only Allah Who decides. In Him, I put my trust. And in Him let the faithful put their trust."

[269]   Chapter 12, Verse 69 of the Quran

When they entered Joseph's presence, he called his brother
Benjamin aside, and confided to him, "I am indeed your brother
Joseph! So do not feel distressed about what they have been doing."

[270]   Chapter 12, Verse 70 of the Quran

When Joseph had provided them with supplies, he slipped the royal
cup into his brother's bag. Then a herald cried, "O people of the
caravan! You must be thieves!"

[271]   Chapter 12, Verse 71 of the Quran

They asked, turning back, "What have you lost?"

[272]   Chapter 12, Verse 72 of the Quran

The herald along with the guards replied, "We have lost the King's
measuring cup. And whoever brings it will be awarded a camel-
load of grain. I guarantee it."

[273]   Chapter 12, Verse 73 of the Quran

Joseph's brothers replied, "By Allah! You know well that we did
not come to cause trouble in the land, nor are we thieves."

[274]   Chapter 12, Verse 74 of the Quran

Joseph's men asked, "What should be the price for theft if you are
lying?"

[275]   Chapter 12, Verse 75 of the Quran

Joseph's brothers responded, "The price will be the enslavement of
the one in whose bag the cup is found. That is how we punish the
wrongdoers."

[276]   Chapter 12, Verse 76 of the Quran

Joseph began searching their bags before that of his brother
Benjamin, then brought it out of Benjamin's bag. This is how We
inspired Joseph to plan. He could not have taken his brother under
the King's law, but Allah had so willed. We elevate in rank
whoever We will. But above those ranking in knowledge is the One
All-Knowing.

[277]   Chapter 12, Verse 77 of the Quran

To distance themselves, Joseph's brothers argued, "If he has stolen,
so did his full brother before." But Joseph suppressed his outrage—
revealing nothing to them—and said to himself, "You are in such
an evil position, and Allah knows best the truth of what you claim."

[278]   Chapter 12, Verse 78 of the Quran

They appealed, "O Chief Minister! He has a very old father, so take
one of us instead. We surely see you as one of the good-doers."

[279]   Chapter 12, Verse 79 of the Quran

Joseph responded, "Allah forbid that we should take other than the
one with whom we found our property. Otherwise, we would surely
be unjust."

[280]   Chapter 12, Verse 80 of the Quran

When they lost all hope in him, they spoke privately. The eldest of them said, "Do you not know that your father had taken a solemn oath by Allah from you, nor how you failed him regarding Joseph before? So I am not leaving this land until my father allows me to, or Allah decides for me. For He is the Best of Judges.

[281]   Chapter 12, Verse 81 of the Quran

Return to your father and say, 'O our father! Your son committed theft. We testify only to what we know. We could not guard against the unforeseen.

[282]   Chapter 12, Verse 82 of the Quran

Ask the people of the land where we were and the caravan we travelled with. We are certainly telling the truth."

[283]   Chapter 12, Verse 83 of the Quran

He cried, "No! Your souls must have tempted you to do something evil. So I am left with nothing but beautiful patience! I trust Allah will return them all to me. Surely He ʿaloneʾ is the All-Knowing, All-Wise."

[284]   Chapter 12, Verse 84 of the Quran

He turned away from them, lamenting, "Alas, poor Joseph!" And his eyes turned white out of the grief he suppressed.

[285]   Chapter 12, Verse 85 of the Quran

They said, "By Allah! You will not cease to remember Joseph until you lose your health or ˹even˺ your life."

[286]   Chapter 12, Verse 86 of the Quran

He replied, "I complain of my anguish and sorrow only to Allah, and I know from Allah what you do not know.

[287]   Chapter 12, Verse 87 of the Quran

O my sons! Go and search diligently for Joseph and his brother. And do not lose hope in the mercy of Allah, for no one loses hope in Allah's mercy except those with no faith."

[288]   Chapter 12, Verse 88 of the Quran

When they entered Joseph's presence, they pleaded, "O Chief Minister! We and our family have been touched with hardship, and we have brought only a few worthless coins, but please give us our supplies in full and be charitable to us. Indeed, Allah rewards the charitable."

[289]   Chapter 12, Verse 89 of the Quran

He asked, "Do you remember what you did to Joseph and his brother in your ignorance?"

[290]   Chapter 12, Verse 90 of the Quran

They replied in shock, "Are you really Joseph?" He said, "I am Joseph, and here is my brother Benjamin! Allah has truly been gracious to us. Surely whoever is mindful of Allah and patient, then certainly Allah never discounts the reward of the good-doers."

[291] Chapter 12, Verse 91 of the Quran

They admitted, "By Allah! Allah has truly preferred you over us, and we have surely been sinful."

[292] Chapter 12, Verse 92 of the Quran

Joseph said, "There is no blame on you today. May Allah forgive you! He is the Most Merciful of the merciful!

[293] Chapter 12, Verse 93 of the Quran

Go with this shirt of mine and cast it over my father's face, and he will regain his sight. Then come back to me with your whole family."

[294] Chapter 12, Verse 94 of the Quran

When the caravan departed from Egypt, their father said to those around him, "You may think I am senile, but I certainly sense the smell of Joseph."

[295] Chapter 12, Verse 95 of the Quran

They replied, "By Allah! You are definitely still in your old delusion."

[296] Chapter 12, Verse 96 of the Quran

But when the bearer of the good news arrived, he cast the shirt over Jacob's face, so he regained his sight. Jacob then said to his children, "Did I not tell you that I truly know from Allah what you do not know?"

[297]   Chapter 12, Verse 97 of the Quran

They begged, "O our father! Pray for the forgiveness of our sins. We have certainly been sinful."

[298]   Chapter 12, Verse 98 of the Quran

He said, "I will pray to my Master for your forgiveness. He alone is indeed the All-Forgiving, Most Merciful."

[299]   Chapter 12, Verse 99 of the Quran

When they entered Joseph's presence, he received his parents graciously and said, "Enter Egypt, Allah willing, in security."

[300]   Chapter 12, Verse 100 of the Quran

Then he raised his parents to the throne, and they all fell down in prostration to Joseph, who then said, "O my dear father! This is the interpretation of my old dream. My Master has made it come true. He was truly kind to me when He freed me from prison and brought you all from the desert after Satan had ignited rivalry between me and my siblings. Indeed my Master is subtle in fulfilling what He wills. Surely, He alone is the All-Knowing, All-Wise."

[301]   Chapter 12, Verse 101 of the Quran

"My Master! You have surely granted me authority and taught me the interpretation of dreams. O Originator of the heavens and the earth! You are my Guardian in this world and the Hereafter. Allow me to die as one who submits and join me with the righteous."

[302] Chapter 20, Verse 81 of the Quran

> "Eat from the good things We have provided for you, but do not transgress in them, or My wrath will befall you. And whoever My wrath befalls is certainly doomed."

Indeed, in the creation of the heavens and the earth; the alternation of the day and the night; the ships that sail the sea for the benefit of humanity; the rain sent down by Allah from the skies, reviving the earth after its death; the scattering of all kinds of creatures throughout; the shifting of the winds; and the clouds drifting between the heavens and the earth — in all of this are surely signs for people of understanding.

Chapter 02, Verse 164 of the Quran